The New Bohemia

The New Bohemia

John Gruen

Photographs by
Fred W. McDarrah

a cappella books

a cappella books
an imprint of
Chicago Review Press

Editorial offices:
PO Box 380
Pennington, NJ 08534

Business/Sales offices:
814 N. Franklin St.
Chicago, IL 60610

Cover art: "The New Bohemia," original collage, by Larry Rivers
Courtesy John Gruen
Cover art photographed by David Allison

The review by Jonas Mekas of *Christmas on Earth,* which appears on
page 106, was first published in *East Side Review #1* (copyright ©
1966 East Side Press, Inc.). George Brecht's *Incidental Music,* which
appears on page 128, is reprinted by permission of the composer
and *Fluxus,* in which it was first published. The quotes on pages
132–4, 136, and 138–9 from Dick Higgins' *Jefferson's Birthday and
Postface* (both copyright © 1964 by Richard C. Higgins) are
included by permission of Something Else Press, Inc. The map of
the East Village, which appears on pages 182–3, is reprinted by
permission of the *East Village Other.*

Reprint coordinated by Richard Carlin

Library of Congress Cataloging-in-Publication Data
Gruen, John.
   The new Bohemia / by John Gruen ; photographs by
Fred W. McDarrah.
     p. cm.
   Includes index.
   Summary: A history of the artistic movements in the East Village of New
York in the early and mid 1960s, focusing on such individuals as Andy
Warhol, Allen Ginsberg, and the Fugs.
   ISBN 1-55652-097-2 : $11.95
   1. Arts, American—New York (New York, N.Y.)—Juvenile
literature.
   2. Arts, Modern—20th century—New York (N.Y.)—Juvenile literature.
   3. New York (N.Y.)—Popular culture.   4. East Village (New York,
N.Y.)—Popular culture—Juvenile literature. [1. Arts, Modern—20th
century—New York (N.Y.) 2. East Village (New York, N.Y.)—Popular
culture. 3. New York (N.Y.)—Popular culture.]
I. McDarrah, Fred W.   ill. II. Title.
NX511.N4G68   1990
700′.9747′1—dc20
                                          90-37668
                                            CIP
                                            AC

For
Jane

Acknowledgments 1966

I wish to express my gratitude to Mr. Clay Felker, Editor of *New York, The Herald Tribune Sunday Magazine,* for suggesting that I write the article entitled "The New Bohemia," published in the November 29, 1964, issue of *New York.* This article has served as the springboard for the writing of this book.

Contents

Author's Note

I recently took a walk in the East Village and did not rediscover my youth there.

How could I? I am twenty-five years older and have long been away from the day-to-day, taken-for-granted, low-budget highs and lows of East Village life. Indeed, some twenty-five years ago, my wife, young daughter, and I moved from Tompkins Square—from Tenth Street between Avenues A and B—to the so-called "safety" of the Upper West Side.

We came to recognize that the East Village, where this book was written and which had attracted us ten years earlier, no longer existed. The drug scene in Alphabet City was escalating. Crime in the once peaceable if desolate Avenues A, B, C, and D became rampant. The night and day encampment in Tompkins Square of peace-loving, guitar-strumming, mantra-chanting, sandal-footed hippies and flower children was repeatedly being infiltrated by posses of motorcycle toughs in search of action.

By 1968, the East Village, the seat of New York's creative avant garde, seemed to implode as gentrification and high rents encroached. The dynamics of this once unique New York neighborhood changed dramatically as its aura of safety and backwater seclusion now entered a cycle of social unrest. For Tompkins Square, often the scene of draft riots, mass meetings, and hunger strikes, history seemed to be repeating itself as the crosscurrents of economic and political tension re-emerged with the Viet Nam War, civil rights, and nuclear threat fueling significant protests.

Throughout the 1970s and 1980s, my "downtown" connection, if not exactly severed, suffered from major nonparticipation. I no longer followed a cultural scene that would travel from hippie to hip-hop, from the bawdy rock and roll of The Fugs at The Dom to the inspired silliness of the B-52s at CBGB's, from Happenings to Performance Art, from Pop and Op Art to Minimalist and Graffiti Art, from Judson Church postmodern dance to street-scene breakdancing, from Janis Joplin to Madonna.

A new generation of East Village painters, sculptors, musicians, filmmakers, writers, poets, performance artists, and choreographers encountered yet another world not of their making: an unwanted war in Southeast Asia, undeclared wars in Latin America, Kent State, Watergate, world-wide terrorism, the Reagan years, the murder of John Lennon and, around 1981, AIDS, a mysterious virus for which no cure was available.

But the creative young of this generation also had their heroes and, like their '60s counterparts, knew how to seize the day. Such anti-establishment figures as Andy Warhol, William Burroughs, Timothy Leary, and John Cage continued to inspire and actively participate in this new underground.

Everyone congregated in a club scene reminiscent of The Dom on St. Mark's Place, but far looser and far more art-oriented. It was the time of the Mudd Club and Club 57, where the crowd not only danced and smoked the night away, but also staged nightly "events," held poetry readings, put up art exhibitions and, in the pre-AIDS years, gave free expression to sex in all of its guises. In a way, these clubs replaced the communal cult love-in pads that dominated the New Bohemia of the '60s.

The burgeoning of an East Village art scene came with a feisty enclave of small galleries opening south of Tompkins Square and along East Tenth Street—the Fun Gallery being among the first to show graffiti art and the work of such emerging East Village artists as Kenny Scharf and Keith Haring. But by the mid-'80s, the by-now internationally powerful Soho art scene had swallowed the promise of this initially exciting phenomenon.

As I took my 1990 walk along St. Mark's Place, Tompkins Square Park, and Alphabet City, I realized that an era such as the '60s contained a *zeitgeist* impossible to duplicate in the '90s. Only such confrontational horrors as the Tompkins Square riots of 1989, where the poor and homeless were brutally beaten and ousted by the police, could now bring notoriety to the area.

Still, it is entirely possible that a new and radical Bohemia could be in the making in the East Village. It is possible that a heightened catharsis of experience might unleash new and brilliant work of every creative genre. Who knows? Perhaps today's East Village young will be able to look to the past as well as to the future and redefine the world they live in, conceiving art, music, film, and poetry with richly innovative intensity.

It happened in my time. It could in yours!

John Gruen
New York, 1990

The New Bohemia

"As for me, I answer that we are all in a state

of frightful hyper-tension."

Antonin Artaud

CHAPTER I

You're in the Combine Generation

The look
of the New Bohemia

*A*nxiety and music, anxiety and dancing, anxiety and sex, anxiety and art—these are the raw materials for a new Bohemia. In New York, as in other cities throughout the world, these commodities run rife, and if we mean anxiety to stand for racial tension, poverty, a simple search for something other than the status quo, or displacement— intellectual, emotional, or aesthetic—then it becomes clear that this anxiety, when acted upon, can release numberless creative and emotional explosions.

In less than two years New York has given birth to a new and radically different Bohemia. As such, it is symptomatic of an international movement in the arts. Its protagonists and practitioners may well become known as the Combine Generation. Its center is known as the East Village, an area that runs roughly from Third Avenue to the East River, and from Houston Street up to Fourteenth Street. A large and relatively unknown park—Tompkins Square—is its focal point, but the area's chief attractions are its low rents and its old-world atmosphere.

Greenwich Village, the East Village's famed and by now far more affluent counterpart, seems to have outgrown its usefulness as a geographic catalyst for the new and the exciting. Rents there are sky-high, living costs are sky-high, and the general tenor of the neighborhood, with its beautifully maintained brownstones, is one of luxury. There is still the main drag—Eighth Street—where bookshops, movie houses, and hamburger joints continue to attract the New Bohemia. But even gay old Eighth Street is being replaced.

The East Village has its own main street, St. Marks Place. (St. Marks Place is actually East Eighth Street, but with its name changed between Third Avenue and Tompkins Square; once across the park it becomes East Eighth Street again.) Umbrella shops, bead shops, hat shops, antique shops, Turkish baths, dress boutiques, old bars, new bars, underground movie houses, dance places, jazz places, and a number of Polish, Russian, and German churches line the three long blocks of St. Marks Place.

At the height of its bustle—on any weekend night—you see the makeup-less faces of long-legged, long-haired girls; bearded boy-faces; old women, their heads covered with small, neatly tied scarves; old men, walking in groups, speaking in foreign tongues. You see young Negroes, walking arm in arm with white girls, who have the look, not of defiance, but of *Here it's possible! Here we can! Here we will!* The fact of the matter is that the East Village abounds in interracial couples, many of them married. They have found the neighborhood relatively free of prejudice and they can walk the streets without being stared at.

Walking on St. Marks Place on a weekend night, you become aware of a rhythm. It has an imperceptible underground beat and you feel it increasing as the night wears on. The rhythm of the Combine Generation is taking over. It can take you to a bottle-party in a $15-a-month loft (records by Bob Dylan only), to an underground poetry reading, to a wild "happening," to a way-out theatrical production. It can lead you to encounters with dope addicts, free-love cultists, Swedenborgians, or white chicks looking for noble savages.

The rhythm of the Combine Generation can rush you into discussions with young artists, young composers, and young film-makers, all of them bent on the demolition of the past. How ironic that this should take place in the least demolished of neighborhoods. Indeed, one of the few aspects of the past which most New Bohemians hold sacred is the old and sentimental architecture that so statically surrounds them.

But the true emblem of this New Bohemia is action—physical, mental, and emotional. The New Bohemia moves insatiably. The most overt manifestation of this need for movement can be observed in the passion for the frenetic, exultant, near-tribal dance catharsis of today. There is no question that almost every stratum of society has been influenced by this solitary, exhibitionistic style of dancing,

The New Bohemia moves insatiably

but it is the New Bohemians who have brought it to its highest pitch. Having finally, so to speak, disentangled themselves, couples are now "making it" on their own, while still relishing the conviviality of the group. This has heightened everyone's sense of competition, and unmasked as well as released a heretofore veiled megalomania. Dancing has become an open war on self-consciousness and inhibition.

The Twist, the Mashed Potato, the Madison, the Monkey, the Frug, and the Jerk—all of them already passé— have acted as a massive safety valve for any number of potentially antisocial acts. So, out of the American tradition of the barn dance, has come a kind of salvation. This ironic tie to the past has its parallel in the sense of frontiersmanship that seems to be an integral part of this New Bohemia. Take its mode of dress: strictly boots and saddles. New Bohemia likes leather jackets, Levis, western boots, work shirts, long hair, beards, moustaches, and one concession to the twentieth-century movie-star complex: sunglasses. The whole thing is like a romantic revival of the wild, wild West. From the single vigilante to the hell-bent posse, they ride in search of something that used to be known as "justice" and "vengeance," but which seems now to be a confrontation with LIFE, which is "out there."

like a romantic revival of the wild, wild West

The parallel continues as we find that the pursuit of LIFE involves the rejection of mother comfort. A New Bohemian is invariably forced to live a primitive life, the basic assumption being that the price of freedom is penury, that metaphysical condition in which anything can happen. And to be where anything can happen—and *may* happen— is of paramount importance. In its heyday, this atmosphere is what Greenwich Village provided, only the style then was the beret and flowing scarf—the nostalgia for Paris of the twenties—or the proletarian, "I'm-just-a-working-man" style of the forties and fifties.

The New Bohemia differs also from the more recent Jack Kerouac "beat" scene in that its concern is with mobility of experience. Its highway leads not so much through the Whitmanian wonderment of these United States, as through the currently more relevant Whitmanian social awareness of the development of comradeship, the beautiful and sane affection of man for man.

Perhaps the most distinguishing characteristic of the New Bohemia is its acceptance of integration as an un-questioned part of the scene. Young Negroes and Puerto Ricans are part of the crowd at the New Bohemian bars. In fact, they move with apparent ease and security within every sphere of creative and social activity. It can truly be said that for New Bohemians every day is Independence Day.

And yet a schism exists. Although the Combine Genera-tion seems, on the surface, to be a unified movement, and although its outward appearance has the consistency of a single genre, it can actually be divided into two groups: the creative and the non-creative. Every liberating movement has its fringe contingent, the types making the scene simply because it represents freedom from responsibility, or be-cause to be a part of it all at a certain moment in one's life is tantamount to sowing one's wild oats. Here, then, are the kids who leave their comfortable uptown and out-of-town homes, grow beards, move into lofts, and hide with a vengeance the fact that a monthly income keeps them safe from the harassments that genuinely face the faction they so eagerly emulate. They try on this style of life like a suit of clothes; when it wears out, or they tire of it, these part-time Bohemians either return to their "good" lives or find a new in-group to slip into.

A far more serious phenomenon within the fringes of the New Bohemia is the dope addict. The East Village abounds with addiction, to the point that a rehabilitation center has sprung up a few blocks east of Tompkins Square. Help is given these addicts, but their problems are far from solved and far from simple. The fact remains that most of the robberies in this non-affluent and heavily patrolled neighborhood are committed by young addicts desperate for a fix. These are the extreme cases, not to be confused with the sometime marijuana-smokers who are very much a part of the scene, both creative and non-creative.

Whole movements are afoot in the East Village to legalize marijuana: "Let's Legalize Pot," "Smoke Pot, It's Cheaper and Healthier Than Liquor!" While severe addiction is a more solitary escape from anxiety, pot-smoking tends to be group-oriented.

Freedom from repression and restriction is a social situation by no means confined to pot-smoking. Free love, and sex in general, permeate the entire environment. The Combine Generation, being young and restless, follows in the pattern of all Bohemias. Sex is one more avenue of liberation and one more medium of experimentation. Today's more group-minded Bohemians form cults that celebrate multisexuality. The Kerista group, for example, is made up of young people who live and love communally. They share expenses, and each other. Periodically raided, this sexual kibbutz continues to exist, albeit under gypsy-like conditions.

the East Village is geared more towards bisexuality

While Greenwich Village has its gay bars and homosexual population, the East Village is geared more towards bisexuality. The New Bohemian rebels against the either-or restrictions of hetero- and homosexuality. Whether consciously or not, there seems to be a need to experience the possibilities inherent in the male-female components that supposedly exist within each individual.

This bisexuality is manifested in the New Bohemians' style of clothing and the length of their hair, and in the equality of sexual aggressiveness on the dance floor. While the masculine female and the feminine male have been elements of all former Bohemias, the New Bohemia seems unwittingly to have synthesized the two. This physical ambiguity seems almost a wish to continue prepuberty, when boys and girls experiment together and are some-

10

times mistaken for each other. In general, the American obsession with youth is unconsciously present in the Combine Generation; the effects, in terms of style and point of view, have been far-reaching.

The fashion industry, ever fond of the boyish girl and the girlish boy, has taken the New Bohemia look to its heart. A recent issue of *Harper's Bazaar,* in the guise of paying homage to Op and Pop Art, filled its glamorous pages with Avedon shots of long-tressed boys posing archly alongside their equally long-tressed girls. Their clothes are haute-couture versions of New Bohemia.

But the impetus of the New Bohemia is also visible in far more immediate and relevant areas. The "happening"—a kind of environmental theater that has become a staple of the East Village—often enlists audience action and participation. Suddenly, the spectator finds himself an actor, an integral part of the improvised event. It should be pointed out that the "cast" of a happening is rarely drawn from the professional theater but includes instead such participants as painters and sculptors who, in point of fact, invented this highly spontaneous art form.

Those who attend a happening are aware that the event can be as unpredictable as a dowsing rod; this is part of the excitement. So they come prepared for anything. The point is that the audience, more often than not, is included in the creative act, and what was traditionally a passive role becomes an active one. The Combine Generation wants people to MOVE!

The new film-makers, mostly young men and women in their twenties, depend on themselves and their friends for the making of their "underground" movies. And most of them are as serious and dedicated as their high-budgeted, Hollywoodized counterparts—if not more so. Once again, their stars are friends and neighbors; their locations, the streets and lofts of the East Village; and their backers, the friendly and patient cameramen, film-suppliers, and dark-room technicians who give them extended credit. Under-   11 ground films are quickly becoming one of the most wide-spread creative movements in the world. And, as far as Americana is concerned, it would seem that the hand-held camera has replaced the six-shooter.

The subject matter of these films is invariably either too taboo or too esoteric for the commercial screen. The Combine Generation film-maker rebels against conformity by focusing his mind and camera on unconventional themes, and often chooses to rebel against camera technique itself. The effort to find cinematic liberation is a direct reflection of the attitudes of the New Bohemia, and the most natural consequence of it is the recording on film of the ambiance that pervades the movement. It is almost as if the underground film-maker were inventing the larger-than-life image of the New Bohemia.

The poets of the Combine Generation live their poems. The point of reference of New Bohemia writing is, in general, the writer's everyday life. A whole crop of underground "little magazines" have sprung up, the way co-op galleries once did on East Tenth Street. *Fuck You/A Magazine of the Arts, C, Mother, Clothes Line, Elephant, Umbra,* and *Nadada* are some such publications—all of the mimeographed and stapled variety. They are circulated almost exclusively within the East Village, and seldom get "uptown." They celebrate all conditions of New Bohemian life on an intensified plane, but the tenor is witty rather than earnest, debunking rather than pompous. These little magazines loathe hypocrisy above all. *Sex über alles* takes up a good many pages, and when they have causes—such as legalizing pot, legalizing prostitution, legalizing sexual inversion, etc.—their words can be immediately grasped by any layman. Deliberate obscurity of meaning is eschewed, not only when championing causes but in creative work as well. In short, the New Bohemian wishes to speak clearly. It does not necessarily follow that he always succeeds, but one of the most characteristic means of clarifying his own

Sex über alles takes up a good many pages

A New Bohemia audience in the lobby of the Bridge Theater

sense of reality is to puncture sham, thoughtless conventions and mores.

The aims of the New Bohemia theater are identical with those of its cinema, poetry, prose, and art. Exploration and experimentation reign supreme in the theaters of the East Village. To begin with, most of them are not theaters at all, but lofts that have been converted into intimate cafés with stages improvised on one side of the room. Café theater clubs, as some of them are called, are run on nothing but enthusiasm, hard work, and hope. No one is in it for the money, and whatever meager sum is collected is contributed by the audience at the end of each performance, to be divided among the cast members. The cast itself may range from one member to fifteen, and the take-home pay, at best, may keep them in cigarettes and hamburgers during the run of the play.

The primary function of the New Bohemia theater is the presentation of new playwrights. That it affords young directors, actors, designers, and composers actual stage experience is a side benefit of these presentations. It is the playwrights themselves who have made the New Bohemia theater what it is: a place where any idea can be tried out on stage instead of on paper.

Thus, theaters in the East Village become sounding boards for plays that run the gamut from the bilious to the bad to the brilliant, from the concocted to the conventional to the courageous. No subject is taboo, no action forbidden. The New Bohemia insists on using any language, any gesture that will, hopefully, intensify the theatrical experience.

any language, any gesture that will, hopefully, intensify the theatrical experience

While the underlying musical sound of the Combine Generation is unquestionably folk-rock—whether it be authentic or hot off the griddle—there are many experimental composers whose approach to their medium is as far out as their imagination will take them. Their music is drawn from the everyday sounds of their own lives. Their great white father is John Cage, and they are con-

14

cerned, as he is, with combining the forces of unconventional sound with those of theatrical presentation and audience engagement. In many instances a concert will take on the semblance of a musical happening. To cite an extreme case, the audience may find themselves "listening" to silence engendered by a group of individuals sitting quietly in a concert hall.

Elsewhere, the "music" may be in the form of silent action; the performers, instead of reading from notated scores, will follow the composer's written instructions to lift an arm, untie a shoelace, bump into each other, yawn, or scratch a head. Such, indeed, might be the entire sequence of a single composition, and could take hours to perform.

Sound, itself, is treated as though it were a physical object to be kicked, thumped, thrown, or handled in any manner the composer or performer sees fit. The "instruments" could include an electric saw, a garbage pail, an alarm clock, or a baseball bat. Should conventional instruments be part of a concert, they are used either to make unconventional sounds, or to produce conventional sounds outside of the expected context. What is more, the manner in which standard instruments are held may be totally unconventional.

handled in any manner the composer or performer sees fit

The art of the dance is viewed by the New Bohemia choreographer as an extension of his own actions, life, and environment. He, too, is bent on cutting the umbilical cord, and he will stop at nothing to shatter the spectator's habitual responses. Again, banal, everyday actions are lifted out of context onto the stage. Preferential treatment is invariably given to stances, movements, and gestures that suggest our conscious or unconscious drives, all of them presupposing an awareness of the Combine Generation's emotional climate.

The music for New Bohemia dance (the word "ballet" is never heard here—it is as forgotten as Zen is) may be silence or unconventional sound or, yes, even Ravel,   15

Vivaldi, or Buxtehude, provided it either underscores or contradicts.

In general, every creative activity of the Combine Generation is marked by the wish to see clearly, to make an image of what it is to be alive *now*, to seek out truths unclouded by useless, stultifying veils of hand-me-down attitudes. There is no doubt that this has been the wish of every new Bohemia, but the current one differs in seeking more to enlist than to exclude. It is somehow simpler to slide into it, the only prerequisite being an open mind about its aims and assumptions.

Behind this difference lies the fact that the audience for the creative New Bohemia is so often an integral part of its creative activities. Moreover, it is an audience whose character is unique to the extent that it does not seek entertainment so much as a sense of participation. Too, it is in attendance less to judge than to identify with, to support experiment in the mutual search for an awakening and deepened use of the senses.

The importance of the physical as a reference point here cannot be stressed too strongly. The Combine Generation seeks and respects a visceral knowledge of life, and seems to treat the brain as simply one more organ of the body, almost as if it were trying to close the clichéd gap between the intellect and the emotions. There is tremendous faith in the unconscious and the uninhibited, as well as in the autonomy of the body.

tremendous faith in the unconscious and the uninhibited

To be outrageous, to be sensational, to be abandoned: these can result in chaos or genius. For the moment, it is chaos that reigns in the New Bohemia because of the undisciplined over-reliance on Combination—of brain and body, of boy and girl, of public and private, of black and white, of performance and audience, of one's inner and outer self—which has not, and perhaps cannot, truly come about.

The movement's identification with the distant American past and its rebellion against the immediate past and

The great dance catharsis: Frugging at Bob Goldstein's *Light Works,* a theatrical event starring "everybody" in a total experience combining film, music, and art

present are still too adolescent and unruly to produce, as far as the arts are concerned, any mature works. So far, it has produced germinal works, works of promise and talent, but no major ones.

What it has created—often stunningly—is an atmosphere in which conventional values and responses can be unsettled or shaken up, if not blasted apart. Living as it does within a set of its own conventions (the inevitable adjunct of any new movement), the Combine Generation comes as a necessary antidote for the poisonous claustrophobia it considers itself heir to.

CHAPTER II

Where the Action Is

The Dom

*H*is name if Fruff. He's my little lamby, my mean tiger, my teddy-weddy bear! I always take him out with me. He's so cuddly and good-good."

The speaker, Carol, is a teen-ager, blonde, pretty, and oh-so-cool. Fruff is a beat-up little tiger, a stuffed animal she desperately clutches to herself. It's two A.M. at the Old Reliable on East Third Street, one of the seamier New Bohemia bars. Dressed in blue jeans and sweater, her eyes hidden by a pair of outsized sunglasses, Carol sways her body to the sound of a rock-and-roll number blaring out of the jukebox. Although she's standing at the bar, she keeps moving away from it, letting the beat of the music envelop her. Her straight, blonde hair keeps whooshing from side to side, and under her loose man's sweater the supple outline of her breasts assumes a mysterious rhythm of its own.

It's dark at the Old Reliable, but even darker in the back room, where a group of young Negros move as if performing some weird kind of ritual. Their arms swing high, and their shouts and claps sound like wild drumbeats. When the music of the jukebox stops, their chants and shouts continue uninterrupted. They seem to be following another beat, another music. Marge, the owner, a short frizzy-haired woman, is angry; she wants the backroom ritual to stop: "They should quit it already." But she's too busy behind the bar, drawing beer and pouring red wine, muscatel, and Scotch.

Just then the jukebox starts up again, and a handsome Negro asks Carol to dance. After the dance she orders a Coke. "I was going to be a nun," she says, "but it turned out to be a drag. So I quit. I'm nineteen, so I didn't get very far with religion. And tonight I'm hung up about a pad to stay in. But I've got Fruff here. Wherever I go, he goes. Oh, I'll find myself a pad. This part of town swings. I guess, one day, if I get enough money, I'll travel. I like to travel. But not to San Francisco; they've got a bunch of squares living there!" Her talk is disconnected, but at the Old Reliable it makes sense.

Two cops walk in and Marge becomes very genteel. "No trouble here, officer, I run a decent, quiet place." But the officers find what they came for. Two Negroes and a white man are hustled out. "Creeps, nothing but creeps and junkies in this neighborhood, and just me they find, just my place!" says Marge.

The Old Reliable is but one of a string of New Bohemia bars, most of them old neighborhood bars dispossessed of their local habitués—the old Polish, Ukranian, and Russian men who for years made these places their late-hour haunts. Unlike some of the gay bars of Greenwich Village, these have become a combination of many worlds, where all tastes and preferences easily intermingle.

The New Bohemians are night people, and they move in groups. You can see them dancing at the Dom, a former Polish recreational club on St. Marks Place; shelling peanuts and drinking beer at the Annex, on Tenth Street at Avenue B; engaged in lively discussions at Stanley's, on Twelfth Street at Avenue B; or having chili con carne and steins of dark beer at Charlie's, on Avenue A. At the Old Reliable, the favored drink is red wine, while across the street, at Slugs, the New Bohemian can spend an afternoon listening to live jazz.

These barhopping Bohemians, be they creative or noncreative, form a microcosm of potential violence, which, more often than not, is expiated by dancing, cool talk, drink, and a "connection"—be it in the form of dope or sex. The most dynamic of the New Bohemia bars has been the Dom, on St. Marks Place. The Dom (the name means "home" in Polish) opened a little over a year ago and immediately became the central meeting ground of the New Bohemia. On any night the large, dark dance floor is an impenetrable forest of couples jumping, twisting, gyrating to the music of a perpetually fed jukebox. Young Negroes ask white girls to dance, and are never turned down. The music heightens everyone's need for action, motion, and

These barhopping Bohemians form a microcosm of potential violence

23

Stanley's

release. The Dom's long and roomy bar is lined with young people whose faces reflect the excitement of the place. The talk is animated, and the sense of exhilaration that pervades the place makes of everyone a potential friend and lover.

The Annex, on Avenue B, tells a somewhat different story. One of its owners claims that most of the types who go there are of the non-creative variety, "just beatniks looking for love, but who gladly settle for momentary encounters with affection.

"Most of the girls in here are Jewish," he says, "and, invariably, their male companions are Negroes. The girls are all in their late teens, come from middle-class families, and have a good education. What they are all doing is 'showing Mother.' The fact is that, while their fathers may reign supreme in the world of business, at home they are usually reduced to pampered children ruled by wives, mothers, or mothers-in-law.

"What these chicks are looking for are heroes they can believe in. Their preference turns to aesthetes who are also noble savages. In most instances, however, they discover that their Negro boyfriends are too obsessed with their own problems to realize their hopes, and the relationships break up. At that point the girls usually leave the scene, get jobs, and, ultimately, marry the dentist their moms envisioned for them."

"What these chicks are looking for are heroes they can believe in"

Also at the Annex was Tom, a handsome white man in his thirties whose experiences and travels have taken him from drifter to chemist, from novelist to fishing-boat operator. He now holds a menial job in the East Village. He has been married to a Negro for three years, but his outlook on mixed marriages is gloomy. Now separated from his wife, he candidly admits: "I thought I had no prejudices before getting married. Now I know I have them, and perhaps more than most.

"Sure we found a place to live around here," Tom continues, "it's really the only place in New York where black

25

Slugs

and white couples can set up housekeeping—even Harlem doesn't go for mixed couples, but that's not the problem. The main problem is being able to live together. I left my wife because I've been inundated by the Negro's complaints and, frankly, I've had it. The Negro wants everything, feels he deserves everything, but does little to earn it. He's got to learn that it's his responsibility. The opportunities exist, like education, job training, etcetera, but he seldom grabs at them."

Asked why he married a Negro girl, Tom says: "In our society we think of a colored girl as an object of great sensuality. When a white man is seen with a Negro woman he is showing the world not how unprejudiced he is, but how virile he is. Actually, most of these men have a great fear of homosexuality. For me, it was a combination of factors. Finally, I became disenchanted with black skin, and it didn't do anything for me sexually."

Tom claims that integrated marriages are destined to fail. "The Negroes I know who are married to white girls are usually unable to find or keep a job, and when the girls complain too much, the men take off. As for children among mixed couples, if truth were known, most of them are a matter of accident."

This bleak outlook was strongly contradicted by Mrs. LeRoi Jones, the white wife of the Negro poet and playwright. A year ago, she, her husband, and two children lived in the East Village's Cooper Square. Though now rumored to be separated, she said at the time: "LeRoi and I have been married for over six years. The point is that it is a marriage between two people rather than a testament, and we were married at a time when such marriages were relatively rare. I have a feeling," she continued, "that today's interracial unions, especially among the very young, are somewhat 'sicker' than they think they are. These kids get married for the wrong reasons. But we know several couples who lead their lives with the very normal everyday harassments that beset any marriage. The

"These kids get married for the wrong reasons"

An interracial couple at an East Village bar

problems are human ones, not racial ones."

Bar life in the East Village is an integral part of the New Bohemia. It serves as an outlet from anxiety and provides the sort of convivial social milieu in which the Combine Generation is most comfortable. While a well-groomed appearance is avoided like the plague, it does not necessarily follow that everyone is slovenly or unkempt. There are certain casual looks that do not always require being a sartorial mess. Such looks might even have a thoughtfulness about them that bespeaks a goodly amount of time before the mirror. Still, the effect is one of total comfort, no matter what inner strain the look of comfort may conceal.

And yet, entering any of the East Village bars, you sense a tension. The music, the drinking, the smoking, the cool, offhand manner notwithstanding, there is always an extra something in the air. It could be fear. It could be guilt. It could be hatred. It could be violence.

As we shall see, the East Village itself has always been an area of rapid and violent change, and the current influx of new nationalities with their own potential of violence seems curiously related to the area's past years of turbulence.

It should also be remembered that, while rents are cheap, squalor is usually included in the price, and poverty has been an agent for agressive tensions. Most of the New Bohemia bars are located on streets that teem with adolescents on the loose. A patrol car is never far away from where the action is. If the scream of sirens suddenly cuts through the night—an habitual sound of the neighborhood —chances are that a knifing, or an assault of some sort, has occurred. We are not precisely in Hell's Kitchen, but tempers flare quickly in the East Village, and sooner or later somebody invariably "blows his cool."

sooner or later somebody invariably "blows his cool"

29

CHAPTER III

The East Village: Immigrés and Emigrés

East Tenth Street between Avenues A and B

*I*n a sense the East Village has always been an area of change and unrest. A brief look at its history explains why.

Three hundred years ago, the East Village was Peter Stuyvesant's *bouwerie,* or farm. According to one source, his original home stood on what is now the south side of East Tenth Street, two hundred feet west of Second Avenue. What is now Tompkins Square Park was part of a salt marsh, originally known as Stuyvesant Swamp, that extended to the East River. This swamp had several intersecting streams that drained into the river.

In 1812, under the leadership of Daniel Tompkins, the entire area was transformed into a defense post against the British. This extraordinary man personally financed the fortification, mainly, as history tells us, because the government's credit was not sound enough to cover an issue of bonds for the project. The British, however, overlooked Stuyvesant Swamp when they made their attacks, and Scarsdale-born Tompkins went on to become an extremely progressive Governor of New York. He tried, among other things, to have slavery abolished in the state. A man of great political and personal acumen, Tompkins ultimately became Vice-President of the United States during Monroe's administration. His last years, sad to say, were fraught with political, financial, and emotional setbacks. He died an alcoholic in 1825, and lies buried at Saint Mark's-in-the-Bouwerie.

In 1833 the Stuyvesant family gave ten and one-half acres, now known as Tompkins Square, to the City of New York on the condition that it be maintained as a public park. This condition was only sporadically observed, and the square went through many periods of turmoil. At one time it became a military parade ground; during the Civil War, it was converted into a recruiting camp. It was also the scene of mass meetings, draft riots, and hunger and unemployment strikes. It was again a place of riot during the panic of 1873.

34

By some mysterious osmosis, these years of unrest seem

The grave of Daniel Tompkins

to have left their imperceptible mark on an area still teeming with crosscurrents of economic and social tensions.

Today, as has been noted, cheap rents are perhaps chief among the attractions of the East Village. Rooms and lofts can be rented for as little as fifteen dollars a month. Such dwellings are located mostly east and south of Tompkins Square, along Avenues B, C, and D. Even the huge, low-income project on Avenue D, with mainly Negro and Puerto Rican residents, cannot be called an exercise in luxury living, despite its view of the East River.

What luxury does exist in the East Village may be found on one lone block, East Tenth Street between Avenues A and B, on the north side of Tompkins Square. Floors-through now rent for as much as three hundred dollars, a price that often includes a lot of do-it-yourself. Here live the last of the doctors, old neighborhood families, and, more recently, artists, writers, and musicians who have become more or less established. These people are not really part of the Combine Generation. Most of them are interested in, but not personally involved in, the merging of the arts.

Most of the artists who reside on the north side of Tompkins Square moved to the neighborhood when even brownstone rents were low, and stayed on. While the location is one of the least convenient in Manhattan—some say the only way to get there is by boat—its seclusion and old-world atmosphere, its lovely park, its tree-lined sidewalks, and its markets, which offer almost every fresh fruit, vegetable, fish, and cold cut known to man, provide a unique and self-sufficient quarter.

Among the host of individuals who are not necessarily involved with the Combine Generation but round out the area's special character, are such unusual personalities as W. H. Auden and Rafael Buñuel (youngest son of the famed film-maker).

36   Mr. Auden and his friend Chester Kallman have lived

on St. Marks Place for many years. It is here that the world-famous poet has written innumerable works, and it is here that he and Kallman fashioned their librettos for Stravinsky's opera *The Rake's Progress* and Hans Werner Henze's opera *Elegy for Young Lovers.*

Rafael Buñuel and his older brother Juan also share an apartment on St. Marks Place. Rafael, a strikingly tall, strikingly dark, and strikingly handsome man, though movie-star material on the surface, is a writer who supports himself doing social work. Juan, an intense and highly convivial person, has assisted in the making of his father's films, but considers himself a sculptor. His recent exhibition in New York of faintly Calderesque wire sculpture proved him a man of talent.

Indeed, the list of painters and scultpors now residing in the East Village has increased appreciably since Harold Rosenberg's article, "Tenth Street: A Geography of Modern Art," was published in the *Art News Annual* of 1958–59. While the East Tenth Street galleries are now but shadows of their former selves, and show every indication of dying out, artists continue to find the area conducive to their work.

In retrospect, it would seem that the entire abstract-expressionist movement, or at least what has come to be known as the New York School of painting, had its inception in the East Village. Franz Kline, Willem de Kooning, Milton Resnick, Esteban Vicente, Joan Mitchell, to mention only a handful of abstract expressionists, all resided in the area at a time when the East Village was only an anonymous periphery of Greenwich Village.

the entire abstract-expressionist movement had its inception in the East Village

Today, artists of every persuasion work and live here, not merely because the rents are low, but also because of the atmosphere they themselves have unwittingly created, in which every kind of work can be simultaneously in progress. Artists who have made the area their home and working quarters for years are gradually finding themselves

37

Artist Joe Brainard in his East Village studio

W.H. Auden

surrounded by whole enclaves of young creative people drawn by the ambiance of the East Village.

Among the many painters, sculptors, poets, musicians, etc., who live here—and it is far too long a list to include them all—are Robert Rauschenberg, Larry Rivers, Claes Oldenburg, Peter Agostini, Israel Levitan, Jason Seley, Al Hansen, Jason Seley, Al Jensen, Fernando Botero, John Button, Howard Kanovitz, Francisco Sainz, Lois Dodd, Jane Wilson, Elaine de Kooning, Kusama, Enrique Castro-Cid, Aldo Tambellini, Richard TumSuden, Joe Brainard, Waldo Diaz-Balart, Frank O'Hara, Joseph LeSeuer, Ted Berrigan, Jim Brody, Ed Sanders, Alvin Novak, and on, and on, and on!

There are also a number of people outside the arts, but well known in the neighborhood, who give the East Village its unique personality. High on the list is Stanley Tolkin, proprietor of Stanley's Bar and of the by now famous Dom. Describing himself as an East Villager "since the year one," Stanley (as everyone calls him) is a congenial old-timer given to talking out of the side of his mouth. A friend of the artists, a shrewd businessman, and a father-confessor to the troubled of New Bohemia, Stanley has watched the growth of the area with as much amazement as other local residents. That he has so wisely responded to the impulses of the Combine Generation must be attributed to his acumen for very early noting the shifts in the area's social and artistic climate.

Jefferson Poland, another East Villager, has made a name for himself by creating the League for Sexual Freedom, an organization devoted to, among other things, the legalization of prostitution. But Poland is also something of a clairvoyant in that he sensed a need for an East Village newspaper, a neighborhood paper that would function for the area as *The Village Voice* does so successfully for Greenwich Village.

The gap has now been filled by *The East Village Other,* a biweekly publication started in October, 1965, by Walter   39

The office of *The East Village Other*: l to r, managing editor Dan Rattiner, founder Walter H. Bowart, editor Allan Katzman, and his brother Don Katzman

H. Bowart, a twenty-seven-year-old painter who gave it a slim, but provocative kickoff with one thousand dollars and an excess of drive. With typically offbeat headquarters located on Tompkins Square, *The Other* currently boasts a circulation of 7,000 and champions the causes of New Bohemia. The style is one of humorous candor and immediacy designed to reach the same mass-media audience that so fervently responds to the folk-rock wailings of Bob Dylan. Bowart has said: "I came to the conclusion that most official journalism was a big fat opinion. Because of the superego conditioning of this society, most reporters are only spewing out status quo propaganda. I wanted an intrepid broadside paper, like *Poor Richard's Almanack* or *The Tatler*. I was ready to gamble a thousand bucks on three issues and now we're here to stay because no one else is speaking for the New Left with laughter.

"My hero," Bowart concluded, "is Will Rogers."

A quick glance through the pages of *The East Village Other* reveals its point of view. Some of the headlines read, "Abolition of Jails," "Illicit Tatoo Clubs," "148 Avenue C: No Heat and a Child with Pneumonia," "Johnson Lies to His Country About Viet Peace Offer," "The Con Ed Con," "Generation of Draft Dodgers." Among its regular features are the comic strip "Captain High!"; a crossword puzzle called, appropriately, "Hippuzzle" (67 across: "It's hairy." Answer: "Snatch."); a monthly "Slum Goddess," cute East Village pinup types; a regular column by former *Village Voice* columnist John Wilcock; and "Poor Paranoid's Almanac," another regular column, penned by East Village poet Allan Katzman.

The paper's first editorial makes a succinct statement, not merely on the validity of an East Village newspaper, but also on the phenomenon of the New Bohemia itself. Under the headline "Why An East Village Newspaper?" Walter Bowart and his associates write:

During the past five years the West Village has grown into a side show of gnawing mediocrity and urban renewal,

41

producing an exodus of its authentic population (young artists, poets, and writers) who have been thrown off by creeping tourism and rising rents, leaving the West Village to professional bohemians, "beatniks", and mad-ave types. The natural migratory route from the west side, bordering the Hudson, was along eighth street toward the lower east side haven of low rent. Today the new "East Village" (a term we have to accept because it draws the distinction between the old world immigrants and the more recent west side immigrants) is the expanding real estate market of sometimes squalid, often quaint and authentic old New York streets that made famous the west village of twenty-five or more years ago.

As the exodus continues it now becomes apparent that the east side is destined for urban renewal and 'civilization'. Before that happens let us make our stand and try to guide its growth in the direction of renovation instead of 'urban renewal' and a sane policy of rent control, slum lord routing, better business, and safer streets.

. . . Aiming at the world in general, we hope to become the mirror of opinion of the new citizenry of the East Village.

On Avenue A and East Tenth Street, just a few steps from the office of *The East Village Other,* you can meet Bowman Brackin. For some years Mr. Brackin has been running the Swedenborgian Reading Room, a hole-in-the-wall that serves as a spiritual haven for derelicts, alcoholics, and addicts. Swedenborg's writings are available free of charge, and discussion groups meet every Friday. A two-burner stove is continually warming starchy foods, and four or five cots in the back accommodate an unhappy few.

Another notable East Villager is Vera Karpis, a stunning Russian-Greek with flashing brown eyes, a sensational smile, ivory-smooth complexion, and long, braided hair. *a leading tightrope performer, she chucked it all to run a liquor shop* She was a leading tightrope performer and traveled with her own company for twenty-five years to appear with famed circuses in the capitals of Europe. But, on her arrival in America, she chucked it all to run a liquor shop on North Tompkins Square with her husband, Robert Hubsch.

Mike Donahue, a retired fireman, is presently an abstract painter of some distinction. He helped organize the rows of East Tenth Street galleries, and invented for them the combined Friday night openings, now a convention of the downtown art community.

At East Tenth Street and Avenue B, an inconspicuous newspaper-soda stand is run by a gentleman known to everyone as Sid. Like the Dom's Stanley Tolkin, Sid knows the neighborhood from A to Z. A heavyset man with score-knowing eyes, Sid observes the scene around him with congenial detachment. In the time it takes to consume an egg cream, an interested customer can be filled in on what's what and who's who in deepest East Village.

Moving along St. Marks Place—New Bohemia's Madison Avenue—you encounter the boutiques that have sprung up to serve a community in search of a style. These tiny-to-small-sized shops are invariably designed and decorated with individual ingenuity. Not one is like any other, and each reflects the imagination of its proprietor. On three long blocks, beginning at Third Avenue and moving east towards Tompkins Square, may be found such lilliputian fashion emporiums as Made in U.S.A., Pourquoi?, Hammond Rutherford, Gussie & Becky, B. Anderson, Something A Little Different, The Limbo, Khadejha Fashions, and The Queen of Diamonds.

a community in search of a style

Prices here range from under ten dollars to over two hundred. The clothes are usually simply designed and stress an easy cut and interesting fabrics. The oldest of the new shops is The Queen of Diamonds, owned by Mary Kanovitz, wife of painter Howard Kanovitz. Its specialty was necklaces made up to order, but it became so successful that Mrs. Kanovitz enlarged its space and scope to include women's clothes as well. She now has a branch in Provincetown, Massachusetts. "If I had my way," says the charming proprietress, "I would never go north of Fourteenth Street. I fell in love with the East Village when I returned after a twelve-year stay in Europe. This neighborhood is the closest thing to Paris."

The Limbo is really a men's shop, but on any day of the

The Limbo

week the premises teem with teen-age girls buying bell-bottom corduroys, pea jackets, and pullovers. The Limbo seems to embody the him-her merger of the Combine Generation.

With everything from floppy Garbo hats to high-lace shoes, the East Village couture shops are satisfying their customers' needs and whims. It is suggested that the up-town explorer also venture into the streets adjacent to St. Marks Place, where more new fashion boutiques are slowly but surely infiltrating.

There can't be a Bohemia without secondhand-furniture stores. St. Marks Place and the environs of the East Village have given birth to a whole bevy of them. Within the past two years, antique shops—mostly of the oak-nouveau persuasion—have multiplied like Tiffany lamps. Among the better-known are Decorative Accents and the Potter Shop on Avenue A, The Elk's Trading Post on Avenue B, Grandma's Things on East Ninth Street, The Place on Second Avenue at East Twelfth Street, and The Oak Store and The Ground Floor Attic ("We Hate Oak!") on St. Marks Place. Betwixt and between are a host of *schmatta,* or bargain shops, a godsend to the poor but sensitive New Bohemian. Whole pads are furnished with the leftover leftovers found in these East Village rummage shops.

Whole pads are furnished with leftover leftovers

As has always been the case, the major landmark of the East Village is Tompkins Square, and it now serves the neighborhood in various ways. To the old-time residents—the Ukranian, Polish, and Jewish immigrants—Tompkins Square is a European park, the center of social life on a sunny afternoon. The benches are lined with old people speaking half a dozen languages, usually heavily dressed against the weather, no matter what the temperature. The women wear head-scarves and heavy stockings; the men wear hats, scarves, and sturdy shoes. One can also find an occasional bum, either sleeping it off or talking it off in the sun.

But none of these people is ever found mingling with

45

the young mothers who cluster around the sandboxes in the park. Here and in the playground the scene is racially mixed at all times. In the early morning, school buses are parked near the huge playground on the north side of the square. Teachers and their public- or parochial-school wards engage in energetic games and make use of the swings, slides, and seesaws. For teen-agers, there are areas for basketball and softball and a circular bicycle path. During the summer a huge wading pool accommodates a welter of screaming, thrashing, laughing youngsters.

The recent encroachment of a Big Brotherly park-renovation plan, typically indifferent to the specific needs of the various elements in the community, provoked a mass protest by neighborhood residents. After prolonged and insistent effort, the community succeeded in getting a plan through that suited its needs. The trees and grass will stay. In addition, by the summer of 1966, Tompkins Square will have its own theater and concert shell, an all-weather recreation room, a dancing area, game tables, shower basins, and roller-skating surfaces.

The East Village boasts a quantity of handsome churches for every nationality and faith. Grace Church, St. Brigid's, and St. Nicholas Carpatho-Russian are architecturally the most striking. Since the Puerto Rican influx, small instant churches—usually effusively decorated stores—dot the side streets and lend new local color to the area.

In point of fact, as long as the rents are low the East Village will attract the poor, the rebellious, and the creative. From more than a purely geographic point of view, the East Village echoes in spirit the Lower East Side of the twenties and thirties, which produced a flow of creative personalities, many of whom became legendary.

With it all, however, the Combine Generation is obviously not limited to a single area. The East Village is only one of many sympathetic locations where it can flourish. Its aims and ideas are being proliferated independently on an international scale. To put it very simply, there is

the East Village echoes in spirit the Lower East Side of the twenties and thirties

46

Tompkins Square Park

something in the air today that suggests and demands a mass reevaluation of every stratum of endeavor. In this century numberless such reevaluations have been in progress, and these have slowly but surely given way to a successive flow of revolutionary innovations and concepts. Every twentieth-century frontier has been explored in an effort to conquer—i.e., understand, utilize, control, and extend—the possibilities of life, space, time, and energy. Science, technology, communications, psychology, and sociology (already interdependent fields), as well as, more recently, the arts, show every tendency of merging. And man, himself, remains as much an unknown frontier as the worlds he explores.

It is no wonder that simultaneity, duration, chance, incongruity, and variability of continuity and meaning—even meaninglessness itself—should preoccupy the Combine Generation. To them, these are the *only* elements stable enough to work with.

CHAPTER IV

"Are you Receiving Your Daily Ration of Passion?"

A Kerista group in an East Village storefront studio

*T*he smells of perspiration, garbage, and marijuana—the sweat, refuse, and dreams of the poverty-stricken—assail the caller climbing the long flight of stairs to Allen Ginsberg's and Peter Orlovsky's apartment on East Fifth Street.

Ginsberg, author of *Howl,* has become the paunchy guru of the New Bohemia. Bearded and balding, the bespectacled poet has shared these quarters with Orlovsky, his lanky, long-haired friend, for nearly thirteen years: three rooms on the top floor, every room a bedroom. The floors are covered with mattresses. A desk, a bookcase, and a few chairs constitute the furnishings. The place is geared for LOVE.

"Come in and lie down" "Come in and lie down" is the innocent greeting. To touch, to feel, is the taken-for-granted behavior, and love is the common denominator of all conversation. To talk about love, to "put down" those who fear it, to condemn those who would forcibly forbid it, are everyday activities in the Ginsberg-Orlovsky household.

This search for freedom from repression has, in fact, given way to a spreading paradisiacal cult known as Kerista. "Love Conquers All" is its calling card, and its basic concepts are rooted in the premise that "To know what you prefer, instead of humbly saying Amen to what the world tells you you ought to prefer, is to have kept your soul alive" (from *An Inland Voyage,* 1878, as quoted in the *Kerista Speeler*).

Both the premise and the cult itself are strongly endorsed by Ginsberg. "Kerista," he says, "sounded a bell that was heard all over the Lower East Side and reverberated to San Francisco as a possibility for a new society. Actually, what goes on at these pads is nothing that doesn't happen in millions of homes across the country.

"I can think of nothing more natural," Ginsberg continued, "than couples dating and dancing. As for sex, the resolution of anxiety is accomplished at the moment of tender physical touch, hand or cheek to breast between man and man, and man and woman. It also represents the

Allen Ginsberg and Peter Orlovsky at home

slow dismantling of the superstructure of sexual oppression that has burdened everybody since childhood. New forms of physical tenderness are springing up everywhere: dancing at the Dom, dancing for joy, and, yes, the rock-and-roll groups, the Beatles—what pent-up joys they've released!"

A group of people were lying on the largest of the mattresses. Orlovsky, his long locks hidden under a knitted cap, was plucking the strings of a sitar, one of the instruments he and Ginsberg had brought home from a year-long visit to India. Ginsberg held forth on the good, the true, and the beautiful. Because he is a poet, because he is extremely articulate and intelligent, his words held a conviction in this atmosphere of ease and sensuality. At one point he reached to a bookshelf for Whitman's *Leaves of Grass*.

"Let me read this footnote Whitman wrote to his preface for the 1876 edition of the book: 'I sent out *Leaves of Grass* to arouse and set flowing in men's and women's hearts, young and old, endless streams of living, pulsating love and friendship, directly from them to myself, now and ever. . . . In my opinion, it is by a fervent, accepted development of comradeship, the beautiful and sane affection of man for man, latent in all the young fellows, north and south, east and west—it is by this, I say, and by what goes directly and indirectly along with it, that the United States of the future (I cannot too often repeat) are to be most effectually welded together, intercalated, anneal'd into a living union.'

"There are political overtones in such a statement that cannot be dismissed," said Ginsberg. "And wasn't it an ironic coincidence that the Kerista group was busted on the same day the news about Jenkins broke from the White House?" Although several Kerista pads were, indeed, raided by the police, others quickly sprang up. The City Living Center, a rented store on East Tenth Street, was the most recent of the places where you could meet Keristans in New York City.

"the Kerista group was busted on the same day the news about Jenkins broke"

Kerista Speeler is the group's official newspaper. Among

its many slogans are "Utopia Tomorrow for Swingers!,"
"A Lesson in Independence," and "Anything Can Happen." The front page of its third issue speaks of the whys
and wherefores of Keristan philosophy:

A new concept of man is being developed by a group of
dedicated men and women whose sole aim, to which they direct all their energies, is the betterment and advancement of
the human race. The concept derives from the most advanced
psychological theories, the most recent discoveries in anthropology and sociology, the most enlightened views of economic
organization. It issues from the assimilation of hundreds of
philosophical, religious and scientific texts, and from the combined intuitional power of scores of young intellectuals.

The name of the concept, Kerista, is an avant-garde religious
movement whose roots are as philosophically scientific as they
are mystical and individualistic. Kerista was revealed to a
businessman-turned-prophet called John Presmont in a theophanic revelation in 1956. Kerista, Presmont was told by a
chorus of voices, would be the new religion of the world;
through Kerista would cease the hatred and strife which today
divide man from man; Kerista represents the actualization of
man's highest aspirations, and a stepping stone to a higher
evolutionary consciousness.

Nothing, continued the voices, could prevent Kerista from
achieving the perfection of mankind. Presmont was informed
he need do nothing to bring it about. By means of the natural
dissemination of his institutions, hundreds of human beings
with whom he has come in contact have been convinced of one
primary fact: that only through granting each person complete
and total freedom to progress unhindered, can the personal development of each human being reach its zenith.

The most intriguing question of modern times is why, in an
age when man has delved into the forces of nature and
achieved mastery of his environment stretching even beyond
his own planet, he has been unable to fathom the roots of his
own soul and learn to live peacibly with his fellows. Kerista,
we believe, represents the breakthrough in the science of the
human mind for which we have all been waiting.

Eventually, the *Kerista Speeler* loses itself in a plethora
of dogma: "There is no other Kerista," it proclaims. "Anyone who differs with the clear-cut views written in this
newspaper is not a Keristan. Utopia is not literature to us,
for we are united—with a lifetime commitment—to create

55

that homeland for hipsters which is not empty air."

The homeland of which they dream and write is an actual island off the British Honduras. The Keristans are planning a mass exodus from the United States, an exodus with a mission: to create a "green paradise" for "a special breed of people."

"Talk yourself into going," requests a headline in the *Kerista Speeler*. And beneath it:

Can you visualize yourself spending your vacations in a pure paradise setting? And on top of the perfection of your choice of this utopian community to spend a few weeks or months in each year, the net cost for room and board would be fixed at the budget price of five insignificant bucks per day. When you think that people spend twenty or more dollars a day to vacation, then you can appreciate what $5-a-day-tours can mean to you. We intend to build a series of neo-polynesian, with our own flavored architecture, villages and ranches right through Central America. The tours will include visits to historic sites with planned safari trips into the interior and boat trips to the islands—and of course, the development of our own island paradises on any such islands which are for sale within our buying capacity.

Should the Caribbean island materialize, the Keristans have mapped out a design-for-living program that would make Pollyanna herself look to her gilt-edged laurels. For example, they are already hard at work turning unborn children into perfectly adjusted beings. The Keristan starts at the beginning: "Kerista is dedicated to the unborn children of this planet whose care will come under our control & love." And a barrage of slogans back up their promises: "The human mind is made not born." "Easier, faster, mess-free care! there IS a big difference!" "The Programed course in self-Love." "Jet-smooth ride . . . new style, new comfort Without changing your natural YOU·. . ." "Superior design for A MAN—They're heavy—and delicate. And they require a lot of handling." "When we say stainless, we mean it." "This is a control center for the first completely automatic process to handle man unmarred through nine operations flawlessly."

The ideals of Kerista are manifold, but all of them are based on Love, Love, Love. Another of the *Speeler* editorials states:

One of the creamiest experiences of life and living is to hear someone say, "I Love You" to you. Long walks and heart to heart talks and laying around on sand by the water with wholesome friends and companions bring you the joys of acceptance and approval, without which a person feels dry and empty. Loneliness is hard. Within Kerista you will see the magic of love effect you and in your heart you will find a desire to give love to others freely as you feel the love of others being given to you freely. . . .

When the fruit of a tree is ripe it has perfect balance of moistness. So too, with life, there are balances of moistness, or creaminess, which makes life a beautiful experience. If your life lacks the creaminess of joyful living, it is time for you to examine yourself and prepare a subjective analysis of your current status as exemplified by non-material well-being. Are you receiving your daily ration of passion? Are you getting a portion of hugs and kisses and tender affection regularly? Do you express yourself in some creative way? Have you friends who·are sympathetic to you and who are aware of your needs as an individual and human being?

Finally, these editorials, long-winded and repetitive as they tend to be, hammer home their utopian goals until the susceptible reader may give Kerista a try.

His visit to the City Living Center should, if anything, set him on his heels. A more depressed-looking group of individuals than that gathered at the City Living Center would be hard to imagine. Any number of young men and women lie around on dusty couches, some sleeping or sleeping it off, others simply sitting and gazing into space. Perhaps one of them will be reading a book, another picking out a mournful tune on a guitar. A heavy air of gloom pervades the premises, and everyone looks totally forlorn, not to say totally unhappy. "Spooky" is the word for the City Living Center, especially the silence of the place. The habitués say not a word, either to the visitor or to one another. And the look of these lounging young Negroes and Whites holds little promise for a movement whose aim

"Are you getting a portion of hugs and kisses and tender affection regularly?"

57

The City Living Center

is to "strip life of the complex nonsense invented by drudges, chastity perverts and single-minded fanatics."

If, as is so picturesquely stated, they mean to "peel the banana's thick skin and enjoy the fruit inside, burn through every layer of paint, paper and scum that hides the rich bare grain and smothers the fragrant sap of the wood of the tree of life," then they might quite possibly profit from a closer examination of the human material they have to work with. The Keristans seem to be poor, lost, floundering souls, with neither personal nor communal direction—in short, a group of sad self-rejects.

Too, an air of hostility pervades the musty premises. Under the guise of integrated love-for-everyone, most Keristans project an atmosphere of suspicion. Perhaps this is part of their effort to keep the crackpots out; more likely, they want to be certain that whoever joins is willing to accept their ways. "When are we gonna make it, baby?" was one of the questions asked a young woman who ventured into the City Living Center. The proper riposte would have been "Anytime you say, baby!" except that the girl was so physically repelled by her never-before-seen would-be lover that she promptly turned him down. "The least those Keristans could do would be to give me a choice," she said. "But they act as if no preference is possible, that it is the duty of a Keristan to accept love from whomever it is offered. To refuse to 'make it' is considered hostile."

On the other hand, another female visitor was aggressively told that no one does anything he doesn't want to do. As an example, the fact was cited that "there's a long-standing virgin in the group."

A female reporter, hoping to get a story on the Keristans, was allowed to talk to a few members but soon found herself being groped by both sexes. The groping, she claims, was impersonal and almost mechanical, as though this were an habitual form of communication.

Kerista seems, in effect, to be all feeling and touch. The

The groping was impersonal and almost mechanical

59

mind is left to dream about how creamy life will be on that "beautiful isle of somewhere." "If it ain't fun, it won't git done," says the *Speeler*. "Balling through life is the Kerista way," it tells the world. And, hoping to awaken its somnambulant followers, its unkempt, glazy-eyed, run-down, lethargic misfits, it entices and bolsters their spirits with such anti-intellectual shots in the arm as: "The books which are filled with literature, millions of them, contain information for the mind, but the information about Kerista identifies with the mystical higher self and cannot be studied in books or in a college filled with book-learned teachers. . . . Happy people stay happy and swing in this hip world without criticising anyone or anything, without protesting and without complaining. . . . Kerista is the real scene."

CHAPTER V

The Four-
Letter Word
and How
It Grew

Ed Sanders at his Peace Eye Book Store

*T*he creative New Bohemian, be he poet, film-maker, or artist, has no truck with the Kerista movement. Allen Ginsberg, for example, is not a card-holding member, though he condones Kerista's "love everybody" principles.

The creative New Bohemian is too busy just being creative. If his "thing" is freedom from repression, he will put his talents and energies into translating this freedom into poems, films, or paintings. His life is based on being an individual, and his social life and personal life are his own business. The didactic, humorless clubhouse atmosphere is not for him: his ego is too strong for that. Though, by conventional standards, his social activities are far from repressed, he more often than not lives out his most violent and libidinous inclinations on paper, film, or canvas.

Among the multi-creative activities of the East Village, none seems more outrageously rebellious than the string of little magazines that have sprung up in the past two or three years: *Elephant, Mother, Nadada, Umbra, Clothesline*, and *C*, to mention only a handful. Although these circulate primarily in the neighborhood, they often boast highly respected contributors who are represented by stories and poems that, because of their "daring," "explicit," or "controversial" subject matter, would never see the light of day in the *official* little magazines. William Burroughs, W. H. Auden, LeRoi Jones, Gregory Corso, Lawrence Ferlinghetti, Allen Ginsberg, Frank O'Hara, and a host of other gifted writers, younger and older, appear regularly.

the four-letter word is never taken in vain

Within the stapled and mimeographed pages of these publications, the four-letter word is never taken in vain, but is employed to heighten the sense of reality that the writer of the Combine Generation invariably celebrates. This, however, does not mean that graphic and frequently joyful pieces about sex are the only material accepted. The percentage of experimental poetry per se runs high, and covers all subjects.

64   Of all the underground publications now in circulation,

FUCK YOU/ a magazine of the ARTS
number 5, Volume 3, May 1963
Ed Sanders, Printer Publisher Editor

"we drink
or break open
our veins solely
to know...."

GOD THRU   CANNABIS

Dedicated to
pacifism, National Defense thru Nonviolent Resistance, Anarchia the
Goddess, Orlovsky's long Egyptian finger, Peace Eye, Hole Cons, Peace
Walk Dicking, dope thrill Banana rites, Acapulqo Gold, Panamanian Red,
Honduras Brown, windowbox freak grass, the anarcho-commio-greaser
conspiracy, submarine boarders, mad bands of stompers for Peace, and all
those groped by J. Edgar Hoover in the silent halls of Congress.

GROPE FOR PEACE !

Cover of *Fuck You: A Magazine of the Arts*, Volume 3, Number 5

the most nose-thumbing is *Fuck You/A Magazine of the Arts*. Ed Sanders, its pink-cheeked editor-publisher, is continually hounded by the police, who periodically confiscate issues of the magazine. But *Fuck You/A Magazine of the Arts* continues to publish. The tenor of *Fuck You* seldom has the sadomasochistic orientation of *Evergreen Review*, for example, which can be bought in any bookshop in the United States and is sent through the mails. *Fuck You* is far more Rabelaisian, and takes potshots at all convention and regimentation, admonishing its readers to extrovert sex, among many other forms of expression. While it does so in a language that leaves little to the imagination, its editorial style is so overtly preposterous that it becomes an audacious attack on the prissy, the two-faced, and the strait-laced. Finally, the men's-room-graffiti vocabulary becomes a hilarious assault, and you relax in the face of such a

a bravura display of pornographic pyrotechnics

bravura display of pornographic pyrotechnics.

Where, you may well ask, can you buy your own copy of *Fuck You/A Magazine of the Arts?* It's not easy. But if you hang around the East Village long enough, someone will tell you where and from whom.

On page 65 is a typical sample of Ed Sanders' editorial style, the title page of the third anniversary issue.

Sanders wants things in the open. In a language the Combine Generation understands, he goads its members into action, almost titillates them into defiance of those laws and assumptions which he considers irrational and out of date. Among his many crusades, the strongest has been on behalf of the marijuana-smoker: "A Call to Action —Stomp out the Marijuana laws Forever," begins one of his most colorful editorials. And it goes on, mincing few words:

Time is *NOW* for a *TOTAL ASSAULT ON THE MARI-JUANA LAWS!* It is CLEAR to us that the cockroach theory of grass smoking has to be abandoned. INTO THE OPEN! ALL THOSE WHO SUCK UP THE BENEVOLENT NARCOTIC CANNABIS, TEENSHUN!! FORWARD,

66

WITH MIND DIALS POINTED! ASSAULT! We have the facts! Cannabis is a non-addictive gentle peace drug! The Marijuana legislations were pushed through in the 1930's by the agents and goonsquads of the jansenisto-manichaean fuck-haters' Conspiracy. Certainly, after 30 years of the blight, it is time to rise up for a bleep blop bleep assault on the social screen. . . . But we can't wait forever for you grass cadets to pull the takeover: grass-freak senators, labor leaders, presidents, etc.! The Goon Squads are few and we are many. We must spray our message into the million lobed American brain IMMEDIATELY! . . .

Hemp is the WAY! We demand the "holy weed marijuana" under our own judgement. When a law is useless when a law is degrading when it prohibits the right to a gentle healthful pleasure, DISOBEY!

So much for Ed Sanders' editorializing. The bulk of *Fuck You*'s content is devoted to poems, stories, essays, plays, and interviews that have in common a strong belief in the liberated imagination. One could almost say that the widespread need for expanded experience could be equated with the current interest in and use of hallucinatory drugs. While some of the material may, indeed, have been written under the influence of such drugs, the tone of all of it seems equally charged, and all of it has an equivalent faith in the intensely heightened experience.

Thus, the search on the part of the New Bohemia writer for intoxicating flights of the imagination seems to be a common denominator, with or without drugs. The results offer a complete range from naïve first talent, to mediocre noodling with hopefully shocking language or ideas, to works of real insight and accomplishment.

Among the latter, the works of Ginsberg, Jones, Auden, Burroughs, Ferlinghetti, O'Hara, *et al*, certainly need no longer be tested in underground publications—they have been through all of that. But their presence does serve several vital functions. They support the aim and direction of the underground writer; they are artistically influential; and, of course, they lend literary substance to publications that search out young writers of talent whose works must perforce be uneven and sometimes tenuous.

Ted Berrigan at Cafe Le Metro

Frank O'Hara

But the appearance of established writers in these magazines also serves *them*. This is especially true in the case of *Fuck You* magazine, which will publish the most explicitly anti-puritanical material. A three-and-a-half-page, brilliantly rhymed poem attributed to Auden, describing, if not celebrating, the act of fellatio between two men, is a startling case in point. A transcribed "high" conversation between Allen Ginsberg and Peter Orlovsky becomes a poetic exercise of the "truth-game," a sometimes hilarious, often poignant essay in the mundane recriminations that can ensue after a thirteen-year relationship. Scorching and insinuating blasts against the political, social, and racial status quo are delivered by LeRoi Jones. Frank O'Hara drenches a homosexual encounter at the movies in trembling lyricism.

The underground literary movement, like New Bohemia itself, is constantly on the move. New little magazines spring up periodically as others disappear. New names make their appearance and others vanish. And there are those who never get published at all. For some of these the testing ground is the East Village's Cafe Le Metro, where, on Monday nights, poets are encouraged to stand up and read their works aloud. At the Metro, located on Second Avenue at East Tenth Street, you sip coffee and are treated to hours of poetic verbiage, most of it of the therapeutic, pretentiously self-purging variety. As for performance, there are very few nascent Dylan Thomases. Frequently they know not when to stop, and then an aura of impatience and frustration makes itself felt.

there are very few nascent Dylan Thomases

Upon occasion an up-and-coming young poet will ignite the atmosphere, or a totally new writer will suddenly cause the room to fall into an attentive and alert silence.

But a far more selective group of New Bohemia writers prefer loft readings, a common phenomenon in the East Village. Four or five poets will be invited to read their works, each with an allotted amount of time, to an especially invited audience. These events are much more or-

Gloria Tropp reading her poetry in an East Village loft; her husband, poet Stephen Tropp, is to her left

ganized and serious, focusing exclusively on the poets and their poetry. A table is usually set up at one end of the loft, and each poet is formally introduced by the host, or the organizer of the program. A few folding chairs accommodate the early arrivals, leaving the rest of the audience to stand or sit on the floor, radiator, or windowsill.

To these young writers and poets, their craft is sacrosanct, and their readings, no matter how tenement-like the setting, have an intense seriousness of purpose. The emcee never fails to announce a list of the upcoming poet's publications, past, present, and future, and treats each reader with the utmost respect and cordiality.

The poets' performances are listened to with equal respect, although a funny line always gets a laugh. At the conclusion of each reading there is applause for the poet; spontaneous applause sometimes occurs for individual poems.

These readings are no loft parties. Drinks are seldom served, and the lofts are tidied and brightly lit. Everyone is neatly dressed; the poets usually wear suits and ties. Afterwards people talk, break up into groups, and leave to go to a bar or to someone's house for a drink.

Loft readings, because they are private and by-invitation-only, offer the poet an opportunity to show the range of his talents before a sympathetic audience. Here he can read whatever he wishes.

This aspect of the creative New Bohemia, the literary avant garde, has produced a literature that insists on unimpeded sensibility to word, to subject, and to form. The only censorship is self-censorship. While this literature all too often gives the impression of self-indulgence and audacity for its own sake, the best of it is steeped in self-discipline.

The only censorship is self-censorship

A browsing, uninitiated spectator often confuses the assault on respectability and convention with a lack of aesthetic and moral integrity on the part of the artist-assailant. What he fails to realize is that the New Bohemian, like previous Bohemians, aims quite deliberately at his misplaced vulnerabilities.

71

CHAPTER VI

"Have You Caught *Balls*?"

A scene from Paul Foster's *The Madonna in the Orchard* at Cafe La Mama: l to r, Hortense Alden (in chair), Blanch Dee (on floor), George Bartenieff, Hector Elizondo, Carl Schenzer, and Harvey Keitel

*T*he tinkling of a bell. A beautiful Negro woman steps in front of the audience: "Good Evening, ladies and gentlemen," she says with a slight Creole accent, "and welcome to Cafe La Mama, E.T.C. [Experimental Theater Club], dedicated to the playwright and all forms of the theater." The lights dim and a performance begins.

You are in an East Village loft that has been cleverly transformed into a spacious café-theater, one of a handful in the area. The curtain rises to reveal a couple in bed. You assume they are in a copulating position, hazarding this guess from the way four bare feet stick out of the sheet that covers them. In a while, the actor and actress get up and begin to play an odd game: crouching on the stage, they make believe they are animals; they bark, yelp, and chase each other; after a moment they freeze in position, as a new character enters and begins to sing, in a loud and quite terrible voice, something mock-serious about the tribulations of life. And so the play continues on its zany way, until the point where the playwright could apparently think of nothing more to say, or not say.

At Cafe La Mama, E.T.C., this not very interesting work by Diane de Prima got a hearing. What is more, an audience was there to hear it, and applaud it. A similar audience will be present the following week. Perhaps it will be luckier; perhaps the next new play by the next new playwright will turn out to be a work of uncommon promise. You can never be sure of what you will get in the New Bohemia theater. What you can be sure of is that nowhere else are the likes of it to be seen.

The New Bohemia theater has been dubbed Off-Off-Broadway. The Off-Off-Broadway houses are located mostly in the East Village, but some may be found in Greenwich Village and elsewhere throughout the city. The real way to distinguish Off-Off-Broadway from its more affluent and more professional sisters is by the absence of tickets and by the presence of a basket that is passed around after each performance. For a meager contribution, anyone may

76

witness the birth pangs of new playwrights, composers, directors, actors, and designers.

Despite its rising popularity, the New Bohemia theater is still very much underground. The press, with the exception of *The Village Voice,* does not see fit to review it, and its importance as an incubator for talent has not as yet been officially recognized.

The economics of Off-Off-Broadway are based more on enthusiasm, dedication, and ingenuity than on cash. Thus, café-theater clubs like La Mama collect minimal dues, in return for which they serve fresh theater and free coffee. The Caffe Cino, in Greenwich Village, operates as a legitimate coffeehouse with a sandwich-and-dessert menu in order to make its theatrical presentations possible. The fact is that hardly any of the New Bohemia theaters maintain themselves on their productions alone. When audience contributions net an actor from fifty cents to two dollars per performance (and actors are the only ones who benefit from these contributions), it becomes clear that everyone concerned must have outside jobs. As far as the producers are concerned, the café-theater combination offers perhaps the happiest financial solution.

based more on enthusiasm, dedication, and ingenuity than on cash

While we are here concerned primarily with the phenomenon of the East Village, it should be noted that Greenwich Village was for years *the* territory in which new plays by new writers could be heard. The Provincetown Playhouse, the Cherry Lane Theater, and, more recently, Circle-in-the-Square and Theater de Lys, among others, have made theatrical history and their names have been synonymous with experimental theater. It was the importance and daring of their productions that gave rise to the name "Off-Broadway." With their success, however, came the sort of professional status that placed them in a category where unions finally entered the scene. Having been forced to go "pro," Off-Broadway has, in a way, ceased to function as a platform for new talent. For example, current Off-Broadway production costs represent serious invest-

77

ments. The Off-Broadway producer, like his Broadway counterpart, is now less likely to take chances on interesting but untried talent and is forced to resort more and more to revivals or other, hopefully off-beat, "sure things." And so the fledgling playwright must look elsewhere for a hearing.

One of the reasons for the existence of Off-Off-Broadway is the fact that it involves no such thing as a union scale, which means that production costs depend entirely on what the available budget will bear. So the novice playwright once more has a place to hang his hat. In keeping with the theatrical tradition of Greenwich Village, the first Off-Off-Broadway haunts sprang up in that area. We have mentioned the Caffe Cino, which is the oldest café-theater in New York. Other experimental theaters in the neighborhood include the Judson Poet's Theater, the Village South Theater, the Open Stage, and the Loft Theater Workshop; these do not operate as café-theaters, but simply as theaters that support the young playwright.

The East Village was bound to have its share of such theatrical workshops. Being newer, and thus fresher, they provide perhaps a wider range of quality. Here the New Bohemia playwright is in full charge, and those who follow these productions are exposed to evenings that alternate between the enlightening and the dismaying.

Wild and unpredictable plays may be seen at the above-mentioned Cafe La Mama, E.T.C., on Second Avenue; the Engage Coffeehouse on East Tenth Street; the Bridge Theater and the Five-Spot Cafe on St. Marks Place; Theatre 62, on East Fourth Street; the Far East on East Second Street; and the West Broadway Workshop on West Broadway.

seldom reviewed, often reviled

While some of these may function for but a single season and others may go on indefinitely, one thing has become clear: the New Bohemia theater, seldom reviewed, often reviled, and run on nothing, is a comer.

Basements, lofts, and holes-in-the-wall nightly resound

Joe Cino operating the coffee machine at his Caffe Cino

with incredible lines, shake with the sounds of thundering tape recorders, reverberate with the thumpings and jumpings of frenzied actors in frenzied motion. Other such places are as silent as a dungeon: no words, no sounds, no action from anyone.

Little old ladies write little old plays about the ridiculous; biologists write plays about the life of underdeveloped fungi; laundromat-operators write plays about the mysterious disappearance of all the bed sheets in the world; nine-year-olds write nine-act plays based on William Burroughs' *Nova Express*. There are plays without actors, without lights, without scenery, without props, without words, without action; plays with movies, with photographs, with music, with dance, with pantomime, with television, with screams, gurgles, and moans; plays about vegeterians, about midgets, about anchovy-rollers, about compulsive fingernail-biters.

But along with writers whose efforts make the Broadway bottom-of-the-barrel look like works of genius, there are genuinely dedicated young playwrights whose search for expression is motivated by one consuming desire: to break the bonds of convention and so give the language and form of the theater a whole new lease on life. In most instances they fail. But when they succeed, the results are apt to be eye-opening.

When, for example, such age-old dramatic mainstays as madness, rape, incest, murder, dope addiction, perversion, inner torment, outer torment, and, last but not least, love and hate, are tackled by such as yet "unknown" playwrights as Paul Foster, Lanford Wilson, Tom Eyen, David Starkweather, Oliver Hailey, Maria Irene Fornes, Rosalyn Drexler, Kenward Elmslie, James Schuyler, Frank O'Hara, Michael Smith, or Mary Mitchell, things are bound to sizzle.

What these playwrights share are startling points of departure and totally uninhibited, if frequently inexperienced, approaches to the "theatrical" experience. No holds are barred when it comes to language, music, costumes, and

laundromat-operators write plays about the mysterious disappearance of all the bed sheets in the world

80

Paul Foster (right) and Lawrence Sacharow at Cafe La Mama

settings. When it all works, the results give credence to even the most blatantly offensive subjects.

Lanford Wilson's *The Madness of Lady Bright,* for example, was a poignant excursion into the nightmare life of an aging transvestite, an obsessively self-deluded creature caught at the moment when reality receded to the point of no return. For actor Neil Flanagan—powdered, rouged, beaded, and perfumed—the play provided a *tour de force* that is still talked about.

The turgid and bleak world of the pervert, the hustler, the addict, and the prostitute was examined by Wilson in his *Balm in Gilead,* which opened recently at Cafe La Mama, E.T.C. Here was an extraordinary kaleidoscope of seamy New Bohemians transported into a sort of *Lower Depths,* as hair-raising and illuminating a journey into form and characterization as any. Wilson, who grew up in Ozark, Missouri, similarly ignited the imagination with his *Home Free!,* a totally winning and credible look into the shadowed realm of incest between brother and sister.

Paul Foster, one of the most gifted of the New Bohemia playwrights, startled his audiences with a play entitled *Balls.* Two Ping-Pong balls, swaying under spotlights, assumed leading roles that brilliantly echoed Becket at his most acerbic and spare. Foster's *The Recluse* proved a chilling insight into the disquieting world of *folie à deux,* a kind of *Whatever Happened to Baby Jane* translated into stunning and creative theater. His first full-length play, *The Madonna in the Orchard,* was a similarly lyrical experiment in the macabre and the brutal.

In Ruth Yorck's *Lullaby for a Dying Man,* another La Mama production, the plot concerned a teen-age criminal whose walk to the electric chair (the time span of this one-acter) awakens him to the realization that he has never experienced real love. The guard and the executioner who lead him to his death become the objects of his need to love and live, even to the last second. Miss Yorck, one-time countess, German movie star, biographer, novelist, poet,

Cafe La Mama

playwright, and grande dame of the underground, handled this offbeat theme poetically, sometimes wittilly; the production, directed by Ross Alexander, was enormously provocative. Ironically, Miss Yorck died early in 1966 after a heart attack suffered at a performance of the Broadway production of Peter Weiss's *Marat/de Sade*, a play she had read and deeply admired.

As Joe Cino has been the driving force of the Greenwich Village café-theaters, so Ellen Stewart, who owns and runs Cafe La Mama, E.T.C., is his counterpart in the East Village. Miss Stewart *is* La Mama, the lovely Negro woman who introduces each play with a tinkling bell. She is La Mama for scores of actors, directors, designers, composers, technicians, and, of course, playwrights, all of whom look to her as the most sympathetic producer this side of heaven. Through her energy and dedication to the young and the untried, she has released the floodgates of creativity that might otherwise have remained untapped.

Neither wealthy nor particularly schooled in the ways of professional theater, she simply felt a need to bring a new theater into being, a theater that is not based on commerical success or failure, a theater unafraid of expressing itself in any terms, a theater where the playwright learns as he does, where he can be involved with his work and world twenty-four hours a day if he so wishes.

She will put on a play of any style, if the seed of talent is there

Miss Stewart is not a fanatic avant-gardist. She will put on a play of any style, if the seed of talent is there. Although that seed has often been infinitesimal, and a good number of the new works have been excruciatingly amateur, she has never stinted on her energy, time, ingenuity, or enthusiasm, and she has given all of her productions the best presentation possible.

Being a Negro, and a woman, has complicated Miss Stewart's efforts to find permanent quarters for her venture. Time and again she met with unsympathetic landlords and license commissioners, and she had to move a number of times before finding her present East Village

Ellen Stewart

quarters, which she has turned into one of the most engaging and atmospheric of café-theaters.

Though increasing in number, the devotees of the New Bohemia theater still represent a small group, as audiences go. It is significant to note that the main interest and support outside of this loyal following come from Europe rather than from home ground. Word of Cafe La Mama, for example, has spread to Paris and Copenhagen and a contingent of playwrights, actors, and directors, together with Miss Stewart, was invited to perform in these cities in the fall of 1965. Each member of the company managed the trip on his own shoestring. They presented those plays that were deemed most interesting, and an enthusiastic press greeted their arrival.

This interest on the part of European capitals for offbeat American theater is manifested in the similar movements taking place in Europe, and it is no accident that the Living Theater, one of the most dynamic New York repertoire companies, has met with more success abroad than here. To Julian Beck and his wife Judith Malina, the founders of the Living Theater, their company's artistic flights were far more real than its business practicalities. In New York the Becks, for all their drive and artistry, handled their finances with the same sense of improvisation that contributed to their theatrical success. As might have been expected, the United States Treasury Department did not see eye to eye with them, and eventually took action against them. The Becks served jail sentences prior to their return to Europe, where they are presently continuing their operation.

It is typical of the New Bohemia that its playwrights have seen drama and poignancy in the Becks' plight. The Open Theater's production of *The Court Trial of Judith Malina and Julian Beck,* based on the last day's court proceedings, was staged last fall by the talented actor-director Joseph Chaiken at Cafe La Mama as an homage to the Living Theater's tenacity and accomplishments.

86

The New Bohemia theater did not, like Athena, spring full-grown from the head of Zeus. Ten years prior to its sudden rise, sporadic and isolated productions occurred in what is now called the East Village. The strongest and most influential showcases were the Phoenix Theater, then on East Twelfth Street and Second Avenue, and Julie Bovasso's Key Theater on St. Marks Place. Both focused their activities on the presentation of offbeat plays, generally by up-and-coming or little-known European playwrights. Beckett, Ionesco, and De Ghelderode, for example, made their appearance on these stages long before the term "theater of the absurd" found its way into the American theatrical vocabulary. Jean Genet's *The Maids* was tackled with considerable imagination by Miss Bovasso's company in the early fifties. It may very well be that her production of this strident and bizarre play served as a springboard for the entire New Bohemia theater. Certainly *The Maids* has gained the status of a classic for the new crop of playwrights, as have other productions of that period. It is interesting to note, too, that while Miss Bovasso, who interpreted the roles of both Solange and Claire in her different productions of *The Maids*, was nothing short of brilliant, a recent revival of the play at Cafe La Mama offered the same work with two young men taking the two female roles—as, indeed, Genet specifies in his directions. Fidelity to the author's intent is an important goal of the New Bohemia theater.

two young men taking the two female roles

It should also be mentioned that the fifties saw highly inventive experimental productions by the now defunct Artists' Theater, headed by John Myers, a gallery dealer, and stage director Herbert Machiz. Plays by James Merrill, Frank O'Hara, James Schuyler, Lionel Abel, Kenneth Koch, and John Ashbery among others, were notable for their untrameled, literate, and poetic approach to the stage. What is more, the decor was supplied by such artists as Larry Rivers, Nell Blaine, Jane Freilicher, Alfred Leslie, and Grace Hartigan, pointing to an interweaving of the arts that is now taken for granted. The plays produced by this company also served as precursors to the dedicatedly "uncommercial" theater currently enjoying such an epidemic of activity.

The present underground theater rides off rapidly in every direction

The present underground theater, as Stephen Leacock would have said, rides off rapidly in every direction. If there is a difference between it and previous theatrical manifestations, that difference is felt in the total disregard for the formalities of theater. For the most part, all conventions are questioned, if not disregarded. The New Bohemia theater, still in its formative stages, may yet produce major playwrights, directors, and actors. Sooner or later it will mature into an accepted point of view, vividly reflecting the Combine Generation's attitude towards life. Its style and preoccupations may be brought into the mainstream of American theater. The signs of its influence are already present "uptown," where a certain acceptance of the zany and the off-beat, as well as lapses of sensemaking, may occasionally be observed. Already Off-Broadway has been eyeing Off-Off-Broadway with what amounts to middle-aged envy and nostalgia. As if to recapture its own green youth, Off-Broadway has begun to tap entire café-theater productions, transferring these to professional theaters. The most spectacular of these transfers occurred in April, 1966, when Theodore Mann, one of the founders of Circle-in-the-Square, engaged Ellen Stewart's "Cafe La Mama Repertory," consisting of six one-act plays, for presentation at the Martinique Theatre under the auspices of Circle-in-the-Square. One month earlier, Lanford Wilson's *The Madness of Lady Bright* and *Ludlow Fair* were revived at the Theatre East in yet another transfer to Off-Broadway.

CHAPTER VII

"From Now on, Camera Shall Know No Shame"

Andy Warhol (in sunglasses, hand to face) at the Film-Makers' Cinematheque; with him are two of his superstars, Paul America (holding cup) and Gerard Malanga (rear, in sunglasses)

No one laughed when Nam June Paik sauntered onto the stage in front of the silver screen, turned his back on the audience, and lowered his pants. No one laughs at such things in the New Bohemia.

It was a serious occasion at the East Village's Film-Makers' Cinematheque, born on darkest Lafayette Street. The exposure of Paik's bare bottom was by no means a gesture of protest. On the contrary, this Korean experimentalist, a protégé of the avant-garde composer John Cage, was offering his public a view of what the new cinema is all about.

He was telling them, as directly as he knew how, that the new cinema knows no boundaries. If it so chooses, the new cinema can remove any image from the screen and place it live before the audience, transforming the cinematic, larger-than-life experience into a physical reality. Thus, the jolt of the unexpected—i.e., Paik's rear end—could, and indeed did cause the audience to respond as to a magnified image.

Paik's rear end did cause the audience to respond as to a magnified image

This, in a way, is the reverse of the current *gigantisme* in painting, and the inverse of the taken-for-granted scale of the film image, which traditionally uses size to overwhelm. Nam June Paik, like artists from time immemorial, chose to let the image itself do the overwhelming, and he did so with the sort of sassy wit that is characteristic of the best of the New Bohemia cinema.

But Paik is not just a film-maker. He is a composer. He is a kinetic sculptor. He is an actor. He is a theoretician. In short, he is the embodiment of the Combine Generation compulsion to be a latter-day Renaissance man of the arts, a man who controls his environment and the world through the merging of the arts.

It is precisely this relentless merging of creative elements that, for better or worse, characterizes the entire underground cinema. A single sentence from a Cinematheque festival program tells the story: "The programs will explore the uses of multiple screens, multiple projectors, multiple images, interrelated screen forms and images, film-dance, moving slides, kinetic sculptures, hand-held projectors, balloon screens, video tape and video projections, light and sound experiments."

Everyone gets into the act. Film-makers are attended by actors, painters, dancers, sculptors, composers, and even critics, all eager to participate in creating a multidimensional cinema and steering it towards realms hopefully uncharted.

The new cinema sometimes gives the impression of experimenting itself out of existence. One recent example showed the physical destruction of the screen itself. What was left was the hollow of the stage and a ladder, which had served the "film-maker" as an aid in cutting away the screen's highest reaches. Still and all, this seemingly interminable spectacle had the basic ingredients of cinema: an illuminated screen, an image in motion (the slowly enlarging rectangular hole being cut out of the middle of the screen by a visually emerging figure methodically cutting away), and sound (the obsessive snip, snip of the scissors).

It is safe to say that of all avant-garde manifestations in the New Bohemia, the underground film movement, for all its deliberate derangement, is the most active and the most daring. While the Combine Generation's fever for joint creativity runs rampant in all the arts, it is film-making that acts as the perfect magnetic center for every restless impulse and expression. The fluidity of the medium seems to have acted as an inspirational drug on a host of young experimenters. To them, celluloid is the magic talisman that can forever hold images and ideas of mescalinean proportions. The projector is their magic lantern, bringing to life the genies of their imagination. And the screen is their "Open sesame!"

The most publicized of the underground film-makers is pop artist Andy Warhol. His affectionate odes to marathon triviality—including the six-hour-long *Sleep,* the eight-hour-long *Empire, Eat, Kiss,* and *Haircut*—are excursions in willful ennui, in which he endeavors to give the word "boredom" a new meaning.

At his best, as in sections of *Thirteen Most Beautiful Women, Thirteen Most Beautiful Men,* and *Henry Geldzahler,* Warhol focuses his ever-static camera on interesting facial close-ups. The image of a single physiognomy unblinkingly staring at the audience for the span of perhaps three minutes finally becomes an intense study in involuntary character revelation. In so relentless a confrontation the human face becomes charged with qualities not usually perceived.

The most probing aspect of Warhol's nearly immobile facial studies is the acutely personal discomfort felt by the spectator as he realizes, perhaps for the first time, the nature of his own habitual visual censorship. It is suddenly too shocking to face the face, and the spectator becomes as involuntarily vulnerable as the giant visage on the screen.

Equally illuminating is the fact that this cortege of head-on heads forms a gallery of portraits-in-time. Somehow, the ultimate effect combines the immediacy of still photography with the urgent and timeless clarity of authentic portrait-painting. In an eternity of three minutes, you become aware of expressions within expressions; these in turn change minutely, but significantly, from moment to moment. A great portrait-painter would scrutinize the subject's face for these fleeting, infinitesimal changes that mark or imply the shape of the person within. It is such marks and implications that find their way into the image that ultimately evokes these mobile complexities.

The living black-and-white image as seen by Warhol (color becomes a mysteriously negative quantity in this context) often suggests nineteenth-century portraiture at its best. A Goya etching, an Ingres drawing, a Degas or Manet painting similarly maintains a cumulative mobility of personality that alters imperceptibly with the spectator's shifting visual response. Whether Warhol is consciously

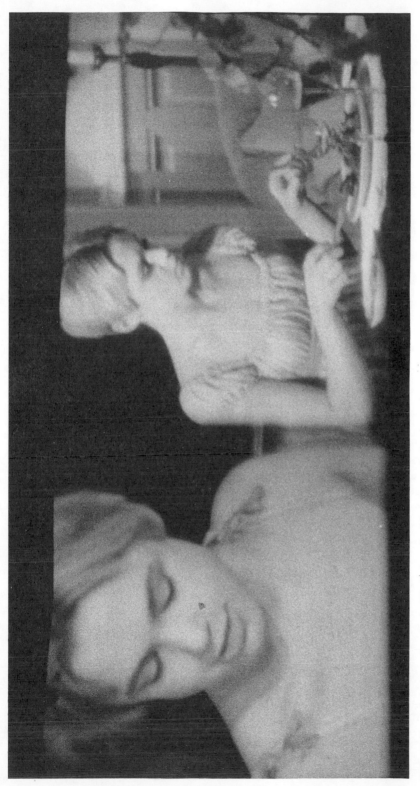

Edie Sedgwick in *Lupe* by Andy Warhol, a double-screen projection; photographed off screen

drawing on these sources is, of course, a moot point. What is important is that in this instance the new cinema is capable of broadening our awareness of the past.

But Warhol has his gayer moods. *Blow Job* is a rarified study of the expressions on a young male face during the sexual act; cunningly, Warhol shows nothing but the face for thirty-five minutes. *The Couch,* a film in progress, is an encyclopedia par excellence on sex combinations. His *Harlot* is a camp romp *à la* Jean Harlow; the role of the "Bombshell" is interpreted by a boy in drag who, during the course of the film, peels and consumes, ever so suggestively, an unquotable number of well-developed bananas.

Along with fifty-seven varieties of instant movies—his "factory" actually produces a film a week—Warhol has invented the superstar: Baby Jane Holzer, Mario Montez, Gerard Malanga, and Edie Sedgewick are but four such celestial creations, shining in the underground firmament. Their thespian ineffectuality and their vacuous prettiness are the *sine qua nons* of their stardom. Both qualities are cherished by the director and carefully cultivated by the stars themselves.

Warhol's superstars are perfect parodies In their way, Warhol's superstars are the perfect parodies of Hollywood's Toby Wing school of drama, and, indeed, they often echo the cinematic stance and gesture of the early thirties. But seeing the superstars in action is more akin to flipping through an endless stack of stills out of the thirties than to watching the actual films of that languorous vintage.

The fact is that the entire underground film movement seems to be high on early movie stills. In most cases the film-makers' fantasies seem to have been ignited more by those glossy eight-by-tens and by the big multicolored coming-attractions posters than by the films themselves.

Warhol's latest enterprise is "The Velvet Underground," a rock-and-roll group whose sadomasochistic syndromes are sung and danced amid light and film projections.

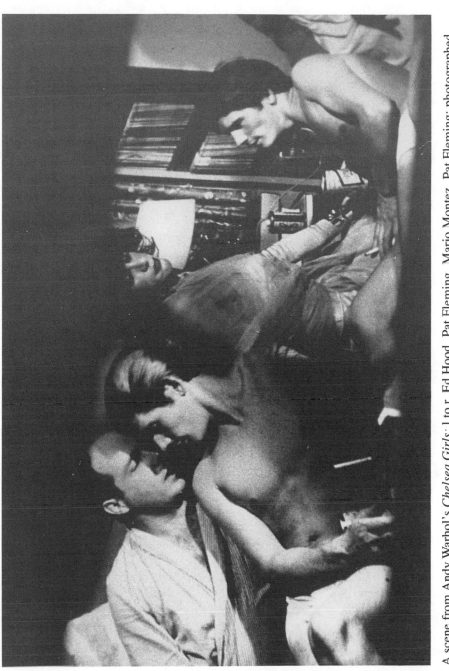

A scene from Andy Warhol's *Chelsea Girls*: l to r, Ed Hood, Pat Fleming, Mario Montez, Pat Fleming; photographed off screen

If Warhol is the chief mogul of the lolling-sex-ad-infinitum cinema, Ed Sanders of *Fuck You/A Magazine of the Arts* could be called the potentate of the "pornies." His three-years-in-the-making *Amphetamine Head* was scheduled for underground release in the spring of 1965, but detectives confiscated ten thousand feet of edited film found in Sanders' East Village apartment. As reported in *The East Village Other,* Sanders commented: "They probably wanted to show them at stag parties. Fuck them! Next time I'll make better films and hide them. As soon as they legalize 'pornies' I'll be the first producer to hit the neighborhood theatres with my now in progress epic film entitled 'Mongolian Cluster Fuck!' "

"Next time I'll make better films and hide them"

It is probable than Sanders' effort, *Amphetamine Head,* will never see the light of the screen, but his enthusiasm for enlisting and reenlisting the services of his stars and supporting players for this feature was undaunted. In one of the issues of his magazine he pleaded:

Will all the stars & super stars of Ed Sanders under ground epic (two years in the making) please report back for certain retakes. The director has been plagued by stars disappearing into Hillside Hospital & Central Islip, & the hip chick star tendency to vanish somewhere in New Jersey. Even though you may have married that dentist, please bring you snatch back for a few more reels of Amphetamine Glory.

And in the same issue:

The Editorial Board of Fuck You/a magazine of the arts announces its first moviemaking venture: MONGOLIAN CLUSTER FUCK, a short but searing non-socially redeeming porn flick featuring 100's of the lower east side's finest, with musical background by Algernon Charles Swinburne & THE FUGS!!

The sexual THI of the underground cinema runs very high. It is one of the most florid of its battle banners, raised time and again as a signal of an all-out assault on the flanks of the right-wing defenders of convention. Sexual syndromes make themselves felt on any number of levels:

the humorous, the turgid, the titillating, the explicit, the implied, the ironic, the witty—seldom the moralistic, unless the battle flag itself is regarded as a moralistic emblem, as much a convention as that of the "enemy."

Indeed, the transformation of sex into a cinematic experience is nearly an obsession with New Bohemia filmmakers. It would seem that it is not only the puritanism of the "enemy" they are attacking, but the puritanism within themselves as well. These young men and women need, somehow, to visualize a sexual Eden as a step towards actually creating one. What is more, their upbringing amidst a miasma of the biblical and parental "Thou shalt not *even think of such a thing*" and the Freudian "Thou shalt not *except in fantasy*" has produced psychological collisions. Shame and guilt have become the goads to hopefully liberating gestures.

In the new cinema, in particular, this obsession often takes the form of an unrelenting search for the magical state of innocence: to peep alone was wrong; now we shall all peep together and there will be no guilt. Film becomes group fantasy. Should a film fail artistically, it will at least have served as psychodrama for the people involved.

To peep at sex was taboo. To exhibit it is just as taboo. But, if the peeper and the exhibitionist come to an open agreement about their roles, guilt will be dispersed. Fantasy laced with fact will rise in flames like the phoenix.

The new cinema is an attempt to *imagine* a poetry of sexual freedom. And everywhere we find the sensually oriented film-maker swinging between *cinéma-vérité* exposés of anatomy and the Babylonian orgy fantasies of silent flicks. Less than a handful of New Bohemia filmmakers have succeeded in translating this subject into strong cinematic statements. When they do succeed, their films, cast as they are with non-actors and set in the most day-to-day surroundings, capture an awkward logic and beauty that are particularly poignant. Moreover, their immediacy, candor, intimacy, and lack of pretention could never be duplicated in commercial films.

The early efforts of underground film-maker Stan Brakhage are a case in point. *Desistfilm,* a seven-minute work in which the camera joins a drunken adolescent party; *Flesh of Morning,* a twenty-five-minute film of one boy's "to be, or not to be" on masturbation; and *Window Water Baby Moving,* an agonizing twelve-minute color film on childbirth, testify to an original mind at work. Brakhage's excursions into abstract vision—*Anticipation of the Night, The Art of Vision,* and *Dog Star Man* (Prelude and Parts I through IV)—have all been hailed as masterpieces by critics of the underground cinema. But, however technically courageous and frequently dazzling, they prove to be highly self-conscious virtuoso experiments and, as such, seem too much like avant-garde textbooks for would-be underground movie-makers. For all their technical brio, they do not make use of the mainstream of his talent.

When double, triple, and quadruple exposures are subjected to rapid, rhythmic editing and cutting, when the eye becomes immersed in a plethora of disparate but juxtaposed color images rushing soundlessly across the screen for hours on end, the effect is more soporific than hypnotic. Only the true aficionado could find these works stimulating, and even then stifled and unstifled New Bohemian yawns are audible at Brakhage screenings.

But back to sex. The color films of brothers George and Mike Kuchar are predicated on one desire—to place sex into the realm of super-camp or bust. Here are George Kuchar's own descriptions of some of their eight-millimeter films, as quoted in *Film Culture,* the periodical dedicated to the new cinema:

Lust for Ecstasy—My most powerful film. A brutal depiction of depravity and crushed morals in a vice of fear.

Anita Needs Me—All the horrors and guilts of the human mind exposed! It reaches deep into the workings of a woman's cravings. Your emotions will be squeezed.

The Lovers of Eternity—The tragic love of a poet of the lower East Side and a girl in a blue nightgown. Stolen moments of happiness in a savage indifferent world.

I Was A Teen Age Rumpot—. . . flows along on a stream of filthy consciousness. Being just a simple home movie about an ordinary family in the Bronx, we weren't interested in an elaborate story.

Mike Kuchar's chef d'oeuvre—and, it is said, Andy Warhol's favorite movie—is *Sins of the Fleshapoids*. It is useless to offer any cogent interpretation of this work, since it must be seen to be believed. Mike Kuchar's words will have to suffice:

> . . . my most movie movie. It is a monument assembled to glorify Hollywood and the "star" image . . . to me Donna Kerness has reached the peak of her "Movie Goddess" image, an image that, in this film, makes her a caricature, a Debra Paget or Dorothy Lamour, that borders on the grotesque, but yet still retains romantic atmosphere. I have given Donna a "leading man" that can only be described as "a gift from the gods." His looks and physique endow the sets like mustard on a hotdog. The script deals with science-fiction while the sets display a sort of mythologic or Arabian Nights flavor. To sum up, *Sins of the Fleshapoids* is my most dearest dedication to commercial American movies, or, to put it another way, it is a joke that cost me a thousand dollars.

"His looks and physique endow the sets like mustard on a hotdog"

Ken Kelman, of *The Nation,* says of the Kuchar films:

> They absolutely avoid continuity of action, logic of motivation, consistency of character or economy through editing, which make for a lack of shape and looseness of effect; largely compensated by excellent color and composition, and gorgeously libidulgent overacting.

The most notorious underground film, Jack Smith's *Flaming Creatures,* has been banned everywhere. Showings here and abroad have met with howls and consternation from censors and purveyors of law and order, and with ecstatic acclaim from the underground film colonies. *Film Culture* was predictably effusive over its merits:

> [Jack Smith] has graced the anarchic liberation of new American cinema with graphic and rhythmic power worthy of the

Mike (left) and George Kuchar

best of formal cinema. He has attained for the first time in motion pictures a high level of art which is absolutely lacking in decorum; and a treatment of sex which makes us aware of the restraint of all previous film-makers.

He has shown more clearly than anyone before how the poet's license includes all things, not only of spirit, but also of flesh; not only of dreams and of symbol, but also of solid reality. In no other art but the movies could this have so fully been done; and their capacity was realized by Smith.

He has borne us a terrible beauty in *Flaming Creatures,* at a time when terror and beauty are growing more and more apart, indeed are more and more denied. He has shocked us with the sting of mortal beauty. He has struck us with not the mere pity or curiosity of the perverse, but the glory, the pageantry of Transylvestia and the magic of Fairyland. He has lit up a part of life, although it is a part which most men scorn.

Rhapsodically romantic critical praise of this sort illustrates the need felt by reviewers of the underground cinema to find cornerstones for their new edifice. They, too, must have their classics. By aggressively declaring *Flaming Creatures* a masterpiece, they are providing the underground cinema with its own legend. The fact that this film was banned helps: firstly, because the masterwork can thus only be talked about, not seen; secondly, because it fulfills the glorious need to be martyred by misunderstanding.

they are providing the underground cinema with its own legend

In point of fact, Smith's *Flaming Creatures* and *Normal Love* (the latter was seen in an incomplete state) are films that attest to his passionate love of color. They have a kind of dime-store-thousand-and-one-nights gaudiness that becomes, at times, genuinely opulent. But along with these exotic images, which often have the jeweled, translucent look of a freshly split pomegranate, Smith cannot resist self-indulgence. The moments of real cinematic beauty and originality are separated by what seem to be miles of superfluous footage. The viewer is forced to wander through bolts of unfurled chiffon *schmattas* through which are glimpsed deeply self-conscious characters gotten up in thrift-shop Orientalia. His films languish campily on

103

location between those sudden moments when all the elements add up to sequences of richly perturbing pictorial and psychological revelation.

A sultry, humid, hothouse tropicality characterizes the best of Smith's work. This slowness, which prevails in so much of the new cinema, produces a genuinely hypnotic effect in the case of Smith's films.

The question of speed seems of tantamount importance to most New Bohemía film-makers. The new cinema is either jet-propelled or else paced at a speed that would lose a race to an inchworm. In the jet-propelled department is cinema-satirist Stan Vanderbeek, whose films are syncopated combinations of slick-magazine images maneuvered with witty animation. The statements of such films as *Science Friction, Summit,* and *Breathdeath* are so accessibly sophisticated as to qualify them easily as short subjects for any art-movie theater. Robert Breer's work is more adventurous: often scratching a rain of abstract imagery on the film surface itself, he produces a speeding cinema based on the movement and rhythm of abstract lines.

The new cinema is either jet-propelled or else paced at a speed that would lose a race to an inchworm

But fast or slow, the new cinema has a catalogue of names that are as familiar to the underground audience as Godard, Malle, Fellini, and Antonioni are to the world at large. Gregory Markopoulos, Bruce Conner, Vernon Zimmerman, Bruce Baillie, Ron Rice, and Harry Smith are just a few who have broken new cinematic barriers.

Some, like East Villager Barbara Rubin, treat the camera as a mute but all-seeing lover. Miss Rubin, a Delacroix-esque beauty given to wearing Delacroix-esque garb, is an East Village odalisque. Her sensational *Christmas on Earth,* which celebrates romantic adventure in exotic places, is not only straight out of the nineteenth-century tradition of romantic flamboyance, excess, and abandonment, but also suggests, at least in concept, a scientific-narcissistic scrutiny of genetalia *à la* Georgia O'Keeffe's "flowers" or Stieglitz' ambiguous closeup photographs of fruit and vegetables.

Barbara Rubin

Christmas on Earth is in two reels, both of which are projected simultaneously from separate projectors; one image fills the entire screen, the other fills the central two-thirds of it. The projectionist may hold color filters in front of either or both projectors. What is more, "the film has neither head nor tail—it can be projected either way." Critic Jonas Mekas, the high priest of the new cinema, described *Christmas on Earth* in these impassioned terms in *East Side Review:*

A woman; a man; the black of the pubic hair; the cunt's moon mountains and canyons. As the film goes, image after image, the most private territories of the body are laid open for us, now an abstracted landscape; the first shock changes into silence, then is transposed into amazement. We have seldom seen such down-to-earth beauty, so real as only a terrible beauty can be: terrible beauty that man, that woman is, are, that Love is.

Do they have no shame? This eighteen year old girl, she must have no shame, to look at and show the body so nakedly. Only Angels have no shame. But we do not believe in angels, we do not believe in Paradise any more, nor in Christmas, we have been Out for too long. . . .

A syllogism: Barbara Rubin has no shame; angels have no shame; Barbara Rubin is an angel.

Yes, Barbara Rubin has no shame because she has been kissed by the angel of Love.

The motion picture camera has been kissed by the angel of Love. From now on, camera shall know no shame.

Cinema has discovered all of man: as painting and sculpture did from the very beginning. But then: cinema IS in its very beginning.

There is no news in the fact that the underground film movement had precursors. One need not dwell on Dada films; they are a matter of record and have been screened regularly and evaluated endlessly. It is important to note, however, that Hans Richter, one of the most active of the European experimentalists, created and became head of the City College of New York's film department in the early fifties, laying much of the groundwork for the cur-

"Yes, Barbara Rubin has no shame because she has been kissed by the angel of Love"

rent New York upsurge in film-making as an area of personal creative discovery. It is seldom remembered, for example, that Stan Brakhage was a pupil of Richter, and that Brakhage's earliest and perhaps best films were made under Richter's encouragement.

Richter, still active at seventy-six but not quite the towering figure here that he has been in Europe, embodies the all-around-artist ideal of the Combine Generation. Painter, poet, actor, designer, film-maker, and critic, he went about his film-making with the same spirit of improvisation and the same desire to capture the unforeseen that mark so many of today's experiments.

We realize, in retrospect, how clearly the current preoccupation—the synthesis of all art activities to produce a cinema event—was forecast in the films of Maya Deren, Willard Maas, Marie Menken, Ian Hugo, Rudolph Burckhardt, Len Lye, and Kenneth Anger.

For sheer cinematographic beauty and psychological effect, the black-and-white films of Robert Frank—*Pull My Daisy,* co-directed by Alfred Leslie; *The Sin of Jesus;* and the in-progress *Kaddish* based on Allen Ginsberg's poem —deserve special mention since they reflect a more conventional approach. The intensity with which subject matter and photography are explored points to untapped resources within a traditional framework, and this in a way seems more daringly difficult than the new cinematic "combines."

The underground cinema, despite its proliferation in avant-garde centers the world over, is still pretty much underground. Even in New York its dissemination moves slowly, and only the most enlightened uptown art houses will, upon occasion, give some of these experiments a midnight screening. When this happens, the so-called sophisticated, ready-for-anything New York audiences invariably boo or laugh these films right back downtown, where, indeed, they flourish best.

One of the most important attempts to educate audiences

The underground cinema is still pretty much underground

107

towards broadening their cinematic vision was made by Cinema 16, a membership venture that finally gave up the ghost after years of valiant trying. Ironically, Amos Vogel, the guiding spirit behind Cinema 16 and one of the most forward-looking of film entrepreneurs, has since become affiliated with Lincoln Center's New York Film Festival, which, in its "safe" commercial way, has yet to deem the new cinema worthy of serious inclusion in its programming.

So, it is at places such as the Film-Makers' Cinematheque, the Bridge Theater, and rented lofts that audiences are exposed to cinematic free-for-alls that range from grueling exercises in boredom to events that are neither cinema, music, dance, painting, poetry, nor drama, but often deafening and blinding combinations of them all.

Consider the recent *Rites of the Dreamweapon* performed at the Cinematheque. It was described by its co-ordinator, Angus MacLise, as a seven-part Manifestation of the Presence, the *presence* ostensibly manifesting itself through "Movement. Light. Sound. Word. Darkness. Silence. Dance. Liturgy. Noise. Stillness." These were revealed by "the Lords of the Dreamweapon—the Dreamweapon of life for the healing of all wounds."

The "Lords" of this extravaganza were a group of young male and female performers in sleazy let's-play-dress-up costumes conducting a confused ritual on a darkened stage. The ritual included endless raga scratching on stringed instruments; the sudden projection of a filmed image on the right wall of the theater, showing a distorted view of a man holding his head; a rock-and-roll number performed at super-volume; a frenzied "dance" catharsis under a painfully bright, rapidly blinking light; and a deadpan, low-decibel poetry reading in almost total darkness: a two-and-one-half-hour endurance test in vain search of primordial origins.

cinematic Kickapoo joy-juice

This kind of cinematic Kickapoo joy-juice represents the nadir of the new cinema. It makes the naïve assumptions

108

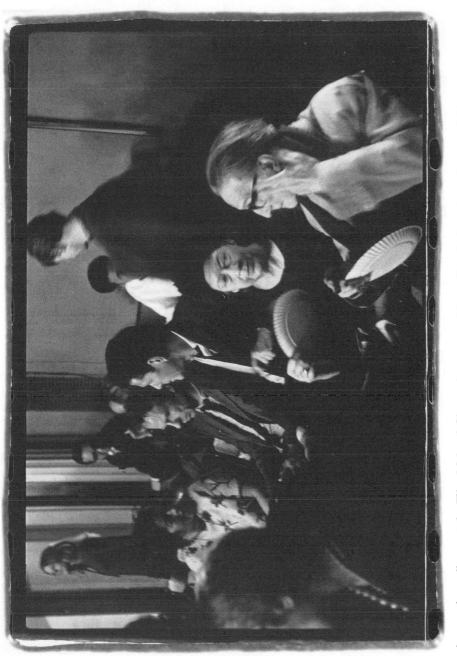

Among the audience at the Film-Makers' Cinematheque were Merce Cunningham (seated, center left), John Cage (to his left), and Marcel and Madame Duchamp (seated lower right)

that the experience of the "wild" requires the elimination of discipline; that self-indulgence equals unleashed creativity; and that getting up on a stage and thumping around will transform exhibitionism into a triumphant revelation of the Paleolithic-man-within-us-all, still prancing around the fire in the caves of Lascaux.

Far more evocative and far more thoughtful are the spare work of Nam June Paik and the productions of the Group Center, an association of experimentalists headed by an East Village artist named Aldo Tambellini. Here the word "experimental" comes into its own.

Paik's *Electronic Video Projections,* for example, echo the stirrings made by the Canadian Professor Marshall McLuhan, the "oracle" whose theories on the imminent "shake-up" of the senses have become a new religion for the Combine Generation as well as a source of thrilling disquietude on the part of the barons of industry, electronics, and advertising. Briefly, McLuhan's message, as described in a recent *Herald Tribune* article by Tom Wolfe, goes like this:

> The new technologies of the electronic age, notably television, radio, the telephone and computers, make up a new environment. A new environment; they are not merely *added* to some basic human environment. The idea that these things, T.V. and the rest, are just tools that men can use for better or for worse, depending on their talents and moral strength—that idea is idiotic to McLuhan. The new technologies, such as television, have become a new environment. They radically alter the entire way people use their five senses, the way they react to things, and therefore, their entire lives and the entire society. It doesn't matter what the content of a medium like T.V. is. It doesn't matter if the networks show 20 hours a day of sadistic cowboys caving in people's teeth, or 20 hours of Pablo Casals droning away on his cello in a Pure-Culture white Spanish drawing room. It doesn't matter about the content. The most profound effect of television—its real "message," in McLuhan's terms—is the way it alters men's sensory patterns. *The medium is the message*—that is the best known McLuhanism.

"The medium is the message"

110   The medium is the message also in the works of Paik

and the Group Center. It was no casual whim that prompted Paik to unreel hundreds of feet of film one evening at the Cinematheque, trailing them up, over, and in between the members of the audience, literally capturing them with the celluloid itself. The audience sat in "wrapped" attention while blank video tape was projected onto the screen, accompanied by electronic sounds of varying intensity and pitch. Paik's program note anent this piece reads:

It is the historical necessity, if there is historical necessity in history, that a new decade of electronic television should follow the past decade of electronic music. Variability and Indeterminism is underdeveloped in optical art as parameter Sex is underdeveloped in music. As collage technique replaced oil paint, the cathode ray tube will replace the canvas. Someday artists will work with capacitators, resistors and semi-conductors as they work today with brushes, violins and junk.

Through this garbled statement may be detected Paik's romantic attitude towards science. Once again we find ourselves standing on the brink of a Great New Tomorrow, which will have nothing to do with the past. And so it is with the Group Center, which informs us that its aim is "to charge the eye and ear with the shifting, changing, exploding images of our time," and that their productions are designed to "bombard, propel and blast the audience into what Group Center believes is the 'New Reality.' . . . The psychological re-orientation of man in Space Era. . . . The exploration of the Microcosm and the Macrocosm. . . . The violent revolutions in our social structure."

Mercifully, the work of Paik, Group Center, and other scientifically oriented experimentalists is usually a great deal more interesting than their manifestos. For the most part—unlike their aesthetic father, John Cage—these young people are verbose but inarticulate, and a wide schism exists between the quality of their creations and that of their writings thereon.

The new cinema, flourishing in the East Village but making itself felt in other parts of the country as well as

a Great New Tomorrow, which will have nothing to do with the past

abroad, is the most fluid, the most multi-faceted, and thus the most volatile expression of creative New Bohemia. Its all-encompassing artistic drives and its all-out assault on the senses stand as symbols of a movement bent on aggressively reevaluating and redefining every artistic precept it can lay its hands on.

Basically, the new cinema's hue and cry is, "Life and Art are One." But the Life in question often seems a hostile fortress protecting a sentimental premise, and the Art a calculated regression into some vague Elysian field in which a band of aging innocents are gamboling.

As for craft: it is almost a dirty word. No matter how ingeniously put together an experimental film may be, it is *de rigueur* that the seams show. A fetish is made of the amateur, "home-movies" quality in the belief that it automatically carries with it a sense of intimacy and familial immediacy, the coziness of a primitive painting, a nostalgia for the hand-crafted, a lack of pretention, the transcendence of the creative urge over the confinements of a schooled technique.

This self-effacement carries with it what may be the new cinema's greatest pitfall: the dismissal of individual character. The new film-maker seems to require obsessively that we find Everyman in ourselves. With very few exceptions, he does not permit us the real intimacy possible only through the recognition of individual idiosyncrasies. He is, rather, concerned solely with group eccentricities, or with the most stereotyped allusions to personality.

Taken in toto, the new cinema appears to be zooming in on the collective unconscious. Archetypal man, object, symbol, word, shape, and sound—all well swathed in *Zeitgeist*—are nudged ad infinitum.

"These movies are like games, not 'serious' at all," writes Jonas Mekas, reviewing some nineteen underground films in the Summer 1965 issue of *Film Culture,* under the heading "Notes on Some New Movies and Happiness." He continues:

They do not even look like cinema. They are happy to call themselves "home movies." Useless, "thoughtless," "childish" games, with no great "intellect," with "nothing" to "say;" a few people sitting, walking, jumping, sleeping, or laughing, doing useless, unimportant things with no "drama," no "intentions," no "messages"—they seem to be there just for their own sake. How irresponsible! Moth wing patterns, flower petals, chance designs: where and what is the "deep" meaning of all this playing? Stan Brakhage, at thirty, and he is still playing with colored moth wings . . . Or Marie Menken: at the Cinematheque Francaise they laughed and made funny noises during her little movies: why did she show flowers, and birds, and fountains? Nothing "dramatic," nothing really for the grown-ups who, after all, are here to do big things!

This is the cinema of childlike innocence, reclaimed with a vengeance.

For all its proselytizing and philosophizing, the new cinema, as seen in the East Village and elsewhere, has come up with one genuine contribution. It has reclaimed from the badlands of the banal, via its intoxication with the amateur (real or feigned), resources of beauty and drama still potent within the habitual and the near-invisible commonplace.

Those who experiment with camera technique—the abstractionists, the dwellers on juxtaposed images, the celebrators of the rushing kaleidoscope—offer, at best, a cinematic decorativeness intended to heighten our visual, aural, even tactile responses. Often using time as though Methuselah were in the audience, the practitioners of this nonobjective plumbing of the unconscious produce epic extravaganzas that would tax the patience of all nine Muses. As it is these goddesses, presiding as they do over their jealously guarded individual domains, must, with the advent of the Combine Generation's all-dimensional cinema, feel heavily put upon.

CHAPTER VIII

From Nouveau Folk-Freak to "Try Some Meaningless Work in the Privacy of Your Own Room"

The Fugs in performance: l to r, John Anderson, Steve Weber, Ed Sanders, Tuli Kupferberg, and Ken Weaver

*S*HRIEK! SHRIEK!
Announcing THE FUGS!!!!

Bob Dylan? Old hat! Barry McGuire? Too wrapped up in "square" causes! The Byrds? Strictly for the! Donovan? This, too, will pass! Sonny and Cher? They're putting you on, man! The Beatles? They *were* adorable!

But the Fugs!!!! They are the one authentic group of singers that has emerged from the New Bohemia, and when their voices are lifted in song . . . well, those old four-letter words never had it so good, and that old rock-and-roll beat was never so gaudily sounded. They hold forth every weekend at the Astor Playhouse on Lafayette Street. Here is a recent announcement about them:

those old four-letter words never had it so good

THE FUGS! An unbelievable group of singers featuring Tuli Kupferberg on farto-phone, Brillo Box, finger cymbals, and various percussion instruments; Ed Sanders on organ, sex organ and Harmonica; . . . Ken Weaver on snare and big stomp Buffalo hide drum; and guest stars. Dances, dirty folk spews, rock & roll, poetry, Amphetamine operas, and other freak-beams from their collective existence. These creeps barf from an unbelievable bag. There has never been anything like the FUGS in the history of western civilization.

And here is "What Are You Doing After the Orgy?," one of the Fugs' songs, music and lyrics by Tuli Kupferberg:

1. What what what what
   What what what what
   Whatta ya gonna do
   After the orgy
   I wanta make friends with you
   After the orgy
   I wanna be friends with you
   After the orgy. . . .

   CHOR: I wanta be your friend
         I wanta be your friend
         I wanta be your friend
         I wanta be your friend
         After the orgy ends
         I wanta be your friend
         I wanta be your friend

I wanta be your friend
I wanta be your friend
I wanta be your friend
After the orgy ends
I wanta be your friend
I wanta be your friend
I wanta be your friend

2. What are you gonna do
After the orgy
I wanna read Blake with you
After the orgy
I wanta eat something too
After the orgy

CHOR: I wanta be your pal
I wanta be your pal
I wanta be your pal
I wanta be your pal
After we pet and ball
I hope that won't be all
I wanta be your pal
I wanta be your pal
I wanta be your pal
I wanta be your pal
After we pet and ball
Why don't ya give me a call
I wanta be your pal
I wanta be your pal

3. What are you gonna do
After the orgy
I wanta go dancin too
After the orgy
What are you plannin to do
After the orgy
Take me along with you
After the orgy

CHOR: I wanna be your mate
I wanna be your mate
I wanna be your mate
I wanna be your mate
Don't care who else you date
I wanna be your mate
I wanna be your mate
I wanna be your mate
I wanna be your mate
I wanna be your mate
I wanna be your mate

I wanna share your wate & fate
I wanna be your mate
I wanna be your mate

4. I wanna be your friend
   I wanna be your friend
   I wanna be your friend
   I wanna be your friend
   After the orgy ends
   I wanna be your friend
   I wanna be your friend
   I wanna be your friend
   I wanna be your friend
   When the orgy ends
   I wanta be your friend
   When the orgy ends
   When the orgy ends
   I wanna be your friend
   When the orgy ends
   When the orgy ends
   I wanta be your friend

These insouciant lyrics, and others—notably "Jack Off Blues," "I Feel Like Homemade Shit," "Wet Dream Over You," and "Caca Rocka"—are available in the mimeographed booklet, *The Fugs' Song Book!*, for sale at the Peace Eye Book Store on East Tenth Street, a shop only the New Bohemia could have invented and only the East Village could contain.

The Fugs seem an inevitable phenomenon of the New Bohemia musical scene. Unlike the ambiguous approach towards sex of other rock-and-roll groups, the Fugs openly satirize fantasies of epic potency. The whining sentimentality and self-pity of most commercial pop music are made blatantly ridiculous by the Fugs who, in keeping with the Combine Generation's attitude towards freedom from repression, have the wit to recognize that sexual idiocies are as much an enemy as is humorless puritanism. Since both the idiocies and the puritanism already form the basis for most pop songs, the Fugs have decided to translate them into the vernacular that is implied in any case.

Thus, their message is as overt verbally as the rock-and-roll beat (and the dances that are synonymous with it) is

the Fugs openly satirize fantasies of epic potency

120

The Peace Eye Book Store

musically. Or, to put it in the vivid language used in the introduction to *The Fugs' Song Book!:*

The Fug-songs seem to spurt in to five areas of concentration:
  a) nouveau folk-freak
  b) sex rock and roll
  c) dope thrill chants
  d) horny cunt-hunger blues
  e) Total Assualt on the Culture
      (anti-war/anti-creep/anti-repression)
. . . The meaning of the FUGS lies in the term BODY POETRY, to get at the frenzy of the thing, the grope-thing . . .
The Body Poetry Formula is this:
The Head by the way of the Big Beat to the genitals
The Genitals by way of Operation Brain Thrill to the
Body Poetry.

"The Genitals by way of Operation Brain Thrill to the Body Poetry"

What it all means is this: The rock-and-roll beat equals SEX, the total body experience. And this total body experience represents the Holy Grail of the New Bohemia's obstacle-ridden quest for a life of non-dichotomized identity, a quest hardly restricted to the East Village. But the New Bohemia, in keeping with its idea of total assault via the arts, uses the clichés of the pornographic to attack obstacles, conventions that it finds truly "dirty."

The Fugs are a perfect and clear-cut example of the process. While they found their first audience in the East Village, their message and style have attracted the attention of some very proper outlying institutions. Late in 1965, for example, the Fugs made a. cross-country tour that took them into what might have been considered outposts of culture in the hinterlands of repression: they performed before assemblies of the Universities of Missouri, Kansas, Ohio, and Indiana and at Antioch and Dickinson College.

The college-level student, with his need for protest, finds that the Fugs and other such "protest" performers are smog-clearers. As one of the Fugs reported upon his return to the East Village, "Our reception was fantabulous!" More tours are planned.

Like the Beatles, the Fugs write their own music and lyrics. Folkways Records have already immortalized them on LP and a new recording company, ESP, has recently taken them under its wing.

In talking of the Fugs, or of any rock-and-roll group, it is necessary to consider the character of their sound itself. Whether attending a discotheque or a rock-and-roll-fest, no one is spared the assault of total noise. Volume per se has become the equivalent of darkness in a movie house. Sound, used to envelop the listener physically, becomes a manufactured environment. Having a quiet chat in even the remotest corner of the largest discotheque is like attempting a conversation under water.

It is a moot point whether the rock-and-roll craze could have reached its present gargantuan proportions without electronic amplification. In effect, current rock-and-roll may be thought of as a phenomenon of electronics, stemming from the public's intoxication with hi-fi equipment and its insistence that performers duplicate the prefab sound and volume that such "home entertainment centers" afford.

It is no news that rock-and-roll has been around a long time, but minus the amplification *gigantisme*. Hillbilly music, folk music, and gospel music have all been lifted out of their small picture frames and blown up to billboard size. Time was when you simply turned up the volume button on your radio or Victrola in order to *hear* things better and to immerse yourself privately in what then seemed a glorious self-indulgence. Today, the opposite seems true, and to listen to music at an intimate volume has become tantamount to a sneaky pleasure.

The aggression of sound, its use as an environment, its insistent immediacy, its power as an equalizer, all these factors have quickened the kinetic responses to fever pitch. The link between the full volume of rock-and-roll music and the frenzy of rock-and-roll dancing is, by now, an inescapable fact. The overwhelming accentuation of rhythm via electronic amplification, having categorically eliminated verbal communication, commands physical participation. Not even the lyrics of the songs are decipherable under the deliberate distortions of style and volume.

Indeed, the entire notion of amplification may be looked upon as a vehicle of assault on habitual response based on "who" you are, verbally. The self must now be defined in physical action, but it is no longer the embrace of a dancing partner that defines the physical self. Since amplified sound touches all, equally, partners need not embrace while dancing; sound becomes the *real* partner.

Amplification has proved to be a launching pad for inter-self flights. As such, it may be placed on a par with drug-taking. As an all-enveloping stimulant, it can create an atmosphere akin to that of the drug "high" or function like an aural LSD. Moreover, the extraordinary response to the throbs of these Vistavision sounds has taken on the overwhelming aspect of *a massive and worldwide "home" addiction to electronic media*. In short, it seems to answer an obvious need for the "enlarged" experience, quite removed from any consideration of the use of drugs to do the enlarging.

Aside from the plugged-in aspects of rock-and-roll, the proliferation of electronics is rampant in all the arts, but, as we shall see, rarely in and of itself.

While electronic music has become one of the major playgrounds of avant-garde composers, electronic sound, in the avant-garde sense, has almost nothing to do with its "commercial" counterpart, and even Mr. Theremin has been left at the starting post. The electronics-oriented composer uses electronics as a self-sufficient musical medium, creating a vocabulary of sounds that cannot be duplicated on traditional instruments. He does this creating in sound laboratories, by means of highly complex transformers and converters. The "product" is a tape on which the composer can further "compose" by editing: splicing for unusual rhythmic patterns, slowing down, speeding up, reversing, repeating, inverting, etc.

124   Electronic music, like automation, does away with the

performer. Although the electronic composer will upon occasion write a piece for tape and orchestra, the purists of the New Bohemia look upon such compositions as virtue sullied.

Electronic music, stereophonic music, electrophonic music, *musique concrète,* and just plain music are no more than so many stultified conventions to the serious Combine Generation composer. To him electrically stimulated sound serves as an adjunct, and only as an adjunct. There is, as yet, no catchall name for the kind of music he writes. His source material includes all of the arts, and then some. Like the New Bohemia film-maker, he wants to synthesize and disrupt simultaneously.

This entire musical scene represents a return to nature, to nature as it is *now,* including *everything* in it: people, things, feelings, industry, science, electronics, the arts, all media of communication, philosophy, psychology, religion, politics, anthropology, mathematics, oceanography, semantics, inner space, outer space, etc.—in short, the gigantic intellectual, emotional, and sociological stewpot we all swim around in.

As far as American music is concerned, John Cage was one of the first to spread the message of creation through destruction and recombination. Music as we have known it has reached the end of the line, and other music must be found. We must look to other sounds, sounds that must be approached and used within new frameworks, frameworks that should be as variable and chancy as is life itself. The return to nature and the redefinition of nature become a return to *sound* in nature, a redefinition of sound as musical expression. Cage has even forced us to *hear* silence, and in so doing has revealed the fact that there is no such thing.

Music has reached the end of the line

But Cage was not solely interested in redefining music itself. He has also redefined the role of the performer, as well as the role of the audience. He has shown how the techniques of the other arts may be applied to music. He has made clear that "presentation" should consist of more than a comely entrance, should in fact involve visual elements integral to performance, elements which may, of themselves, be "musical." He has insisted, again and again, on the validity of the visual as an essential. He has so thoroughly paved the way for musical reorientation in American avant-garde circles that he is now considered a classicist of the genre.

Having cleared a new domain, having given preferential treatment to elements heretofore considered unusable—not to say contradictory or even destructive to serious music—Cage has enthroned chance and variability. They reign still and command the voluntary, fanatical allegiance of scores of young knights-errant the world over.

Cage has enthroned chance and variability

These are the composers and performers of the Combine Generation, a group that includes many nationalities. Some of them found their first audiences in the East Village, although since the late fifties they, too, have had the same kind of small but dedicated European following enjoyed by the new cinema and the experimental theater. Today, the notion of "underground" *anything* is valid only if one conceives of it as an international subway system.

Among the American contingent of New Bohemia composers who studied with John Cage when he held classes at the New School for Social Research in the late fifties, are Al Hansen, Richard Maxfield, Dick Higgins, George Brecht, and Allan Kaprow. They found his teachings both stimulating and eye-opening and readily accepted his views on indeterminacy and the autonomous behavior of simultaneous events (a lot of unrelated things going on at once). Through him they were able to confirm and extend their own areas of interest, including the notions that music should be anti-virtuosity, anti-entertainment, anti-set-performance, anti-set-content, and anti-set-duration.

The majority of the New Bohemia composers have had extensive musical education and training. Many of the

John Cage's *Theater Piece*, featuring Charlotte Moorman playing a human cello (a string held by Nam June Paik); Lawrence Alloway (seated, with crossed hands) watches the proceedings

most "outrageous" ones were music students of extraordinary brilliance and accomplishment. In other words, their preoccupation with this highly offbeat approach to music has nothing to do with incompetence.

Here is *Incidental Music,* a composition by George Brecht, a most gifted artist-composer:

Five Piano Pieces, any number playable successively or simultaneously, in any order or combination, with one another and with other pieces.

1. The piano seat is tilted on its base and brought to rest against a part of the piano.
2. Wooden blocks. A single block is placed inside the piano. A block is placed upon this block, then a third upon the second and so forth, singly, until at least one block falls from the column.
3. Photographing the piano situation.
4. Three dried peas or beans are dropped, one after another, onto the keyboard. Each such seed remaining on the keyboard is attached to the key or keys nearest it with a single piece of pressure-sensitive tape.
5. The piano seat is suitably arranged and the performer seats himself.

This is the extent of the composition. Sound is a matter of pure accident. *Ladder,* another of Brecht's compositions, goes like this:

> Paint a single straight ladder white
> Paint the bottom rung black
> Distribute spectral colors on the rungs between

Brecht's *Saxophone Solo* has but one instruction:

Trumpet

The Japanese Yoko Ono is another highly esteemed New Bohemia composer. Her compositions have the transcendental quality of haiku poetry:

WOOD PIECE

> Use any piece of wood
> Make different sounds by using different
> Angles of your hand in hitting it. (a)
> Make different sounds by hitting
> Different parts of it. (b)

WALKING PIECE

Walk in the footsteps of the person
in front.
1. on ground
2. in mud
3. in snow
4. on ice
5. in water
Try not to make sounds.

LAUGH PIECE

Keep laughing a week.

CITY PIECE

Walk all over the city with an empty
baby carriage.

VOICE PIECE FOR SOPRANO
to Simone Morris

Scream.
1. against the wind
2. against the wall
3. against the sky

DAWN PIECE

Take the first word that comes across
your mind.
Repeat the word until dawn.

"Keep laughing a week"

Miss Ono defines her work as "insound" or "instructure." Insound, as she put it, is a practice as much as a form
of music, and most of the insound pieces are spread by
word of mouth. In effect, they are to be read to others or
to oneself, thought about, and, if possible, performed. The
"score" is the instruction itself.

Instructure is described as "Something that emerged
from instruction and yet not quite emerged—not quite
structured—never quite structured . . . like an unfinished
church with a sky ceiling."

A far more elaborate set of instructions, intended for
definite performance, was followed at a recent concert
at the Bridge Theater in the East Village. This was a
work entitled *Don't Trade Here* by Giuseppe Chiari.

129

Again, the "score" comprises three pages of instructions written in pseudo-verse form, as follows:

You must repeat 122 times the sentence:
DON'T TRADE HERE! . . . OWNERS OF THIS BUSI-
NESS SURRENDERED TO THE RACE MIXERS.
At every repetition
draw a mark
on a long table in view of the public;
The marks can have any shape you like
and be different the one from the other.

These repetitions last altogether 10 minutes.

Immediately. At the end of the 122 repetitions
rub out the table.
Write, with violent gesture:

MILANO TEATRO LA SCALA

SOIUZ SOVETSKICH KOMPOSITOROV S.S.S.R.
KOMISSIJA MUZIKALNOI KRITIKI
SOVETSKAJA MUZIKA TEORETICESKIE I KRITICES-
KIE STATI

THE NAME OF THE PERFORMER

LOVE

Afterwards

Shout. Complain. Like a beast.

Take a microphone. Bring it near your throat.

Play with the intensity level of three amplifiers.
Arriving alternatively and simultaneously at such high level
as to cause very sharp frequencies in this loud speaker.
Reduce to lowest the level of the amplifier.

Vomit.
Or cry
Cause the vomiting or the tears mechanically or chemically.

Silence.

Cause grave disturbance in one of the sets by means of an
irregular contact.

Afterwards.

Take on oscillator.
Transmit in the hall a sinusoidale wave on a frequency of
20.000 cycles every second.

Turned toward the audience, announce:

"A sinusoidale wave on the frequency of 20.000 cycles every
second,

*"Cause the
vomiting or
the tears
mechanically
or chemically"*

sent by an oscillator, is circulating in this hall."
"The wave can not be heard by man."
"Gradually lessen the waves frequency until it reaches a zone.
—between 16.000 and 14.000 cycles approximately—where it will
be heard."
"The hearing is in inverse proportion to the age of the audience.
It lessens as the age increases."
Stroll amongst the audience.
Slowly lessen the frequency.
Do not speak. No expression on your face.
Do not answer possible reactions or interferences from the audience.
Confine yourselves to inform on the lessening of the frequency
every thousand units.
"19.000 . . . 18.000 . . . 17.000 . . . 16.000 . . ."
Arrived at 12,000 cycles shut off the broadcasting.

Chiari's *Don't Trade Here* was not a howling success, but the audience sat attentively through it.

One of the most prolific and inventive of the New Bohemia composers is Nam June Paik, as active in music as he is in the new cinema. His compositions are charged with typical New Bohemia audacity. Here are two works.

YOUNG PENIS SYMPHONY

. . . curtain up . . .

The audience sees only a huge piece of white paper stretched across the whole stage mouth, from the ceiling to the floor and from the left to the right wing. Behind this paper, on the stage, stand ten young men . . . . ready.

. . . . after a while . . . .

The first sticks his penis out through the paper
to the audience . . .
The second sticks his penis out through the paper
to the audience . . .
The third sticks his penis out through the paper
to the audience . . .
The fourth sticks his penis out through the paper
to the audience . . .

131

The fifth sticks his penis out through the paper
to the audience . . .
The sixth sticks his penis out through the paper
to the audience . . .
The seventh sticks his penis out through the paper
to the audience . . .
The eighth sticks his penis out through the paper
to the audience . . .
The ninth sticks his penis out through the paper
to the audience . . .
The tenth sticks his penis out through the paper
to the audience . . .

Expected world premier about 1984 A.D.
Ref. Taiyono Kisetzu: Ishihara

SERENADE FOR ALISON

Take off a pair of yellow panties, and put them on the wall.
Take off a pair of white-lace panties, and look at the audi-
ence through them.
Take off a pair of red panties, and put them in the vest
pocket of a gentleman.
Take off a pair of light-blue panties, and wipe the sweat off
the forehead of an old gentleman.
Take off a pair of violet panties, and pull them over the
head of a snob.
Take off a pair of nylon panties, and stuff them in the
mouth of a music critic.
Take off a pair of black-lace panties, and stuff them in the
mouth of the second music critic.
Take off a pair of blood-stained panties, and stuff them in
the mouth of the worst music critic.
Take off a pair of green panties, and make an omelette-
surprise with them.

. . . . continue . . . .

*"show them
that you have
no more
panties on"*

If possible, show them that you have no more panties on.

Dick Higgins is one of the most articulate of the New
Bohemia composer-writers. The detailed instructions he
gives for his composition *Clown's Way*—a drama in three
hundred acts—aptly illuminate the Combine Generation's
obsessive need for deifying banal actions and sounds:

Clown's Way consists of any performance that uses the information given in the three hundred acts below. For example, one
kind of performance might consist of a performer doing an act
a day for the larger part of a year, without audience, and with-

132

out other performers, bypassing acts that require more than one performer.

One suggested form of performance consists of this: the performers select a performance area, which allows an audience to witness the acts. The acts are cut up and pasted on index cards. These cards are drawn and followed by any performer who has nothing indicated to do. A performer who particularly wants to do an act himself initials the card. Then the person who is drawing cards notices that he has drawn someone else's card, and he takes it to him, returns, and draws again, until he gets a card he can take for himself. Similarly, if a performer feels that an act is particularly unsuited to him, he may place it into the pack and draw again. Some acts are pasted to a card together, and described as two acts each of which contain an A and a B. Before performance, all the B parts are assigned to appropriate performers, and A parts are determined by whoever draws them (if he is capable of performing the act.)

All the props, listed after the acts, are collected onto central tables (or buggies), except the ladders and similar large objects, which are out of the way and on the floor.

When a performer draws a card, he may do what is indicated on it after the prescribed amount of time pause. After his performance of the act he may wait as long as he cares to without drawing a new card. The performance begins with the drawing of the first card and continues until all the cards are used up or nobody cares to perform anymore. Performers may stop and withdraw from performance at any time, and they may return at anytime also. But they can be called back into performance when they are to be included in one of the double acts. Cards, once consulted, are placed into a discard box. Unread cards are kept in a pile with the props. Cards are often shuffled.

Here, out of the three hundred acts, are five picked at random. Time durations are specified for each of them:

Act Thirty-Seven 20″ Take a coin and toss it. Look to see whether you've thrown heads or tails. If you have thrown heads, pocket the coin. If you have thrown tails, retire from the performance and join the audience.

Act Fifty-Four 50″ Vibrate violently.

Act Ninety-Five 40″ Get pretty sexy with somebody.

Act One Hundred and Ninety-Four 40″ Notice any portable object as far across the performance area as possible. Go to it. Pick it up. Laugh, first happily, then very sadly: "Ha ha ha haw haw haw haw aw aww awrgh h h h . . . " for example. Make it clear that you are about to cry. Do not cry. Sit down a while.

Act Two Hundred and Eighteen 10" Say loudly and rapidly, "We si ray cop the sur tab my the no the a a ing at yes so sure ly waw much tell a he know are in and cats, poo you fran cop ly un one nick pass dyuh pah ver cop war das sil in France swly ikh mor ex fur veer enn dee and ly der."

Higgins has composed hundreds of compositions, most of them of this variety.

In the East Village's Pocket Theatre, one of the most flamboyant in the group, California-born La Monte Young, offered his *Dream Music,* "A Light Sound Production." Basically, Young believes that music has neither a beginning nor an end; his ideal is to sustain one chord eternally. On the occasion of the Pocket Theatre concert, the audience sat in near-darkness observing the dimly lighted stage. On its floor could be made out four figures sitting cross-legged in a row. The sight suggested a contemplation scene in a Buddhist temple. As the eyes became adjusted to the dimness, it was possible to notice slight hand activity on the part of two of the performers. They appeared to be bowing stringed instruments.

his ideal is to sustain one chord eternally

The sound emitted, which was obviously shaped by amplification, seemed to be a sustained drone, of one constant pitch held ad infinitum. It became clear, eventually, that the string tone was being abetted by the human voice lending infinitesimal variation to the "interior" of the sound. This sustained chord lasted for hours, not nearly long enough for Young.

Writing in *The Village Voice* about the music of La Monte Young, Jill Johnston said:

As a composer he has always been involved with things that go on a long time, and he says that his longest performed piece was one of the Dreams from *Four Dreams of China.* This piece began at George Segal's farm nearly two years ago, and since silences were included in the composition, and the last silence could continue for an indefinite period of time, the *Dream* is still going on and presumably it will endure forever.

134

LaMonte Young's *Theater of Eternal Music*, presented at the Film-Makers' Cinematheque: l to r, Tony Conrad, LaMonte Young, Marion Zazeela, and John Cale

One of Young's exquisite ideas for eliminating mortal anxiety is the erection of Dream Houses in which performances of this type would be going on continuously in various rooms. One could visit, or reside as a recluse in this "living musical organism."

Young, who recently won a Guggenheim fellowship, is not interested only in this hypnotic form of musical continuum. He has long experimented with interminable sounds of an unbearable nature, as in a duet involving a gong dragged over a cement floor and a wastebasket scraped against a wall.

Although the foregoing examples offer but a limited sampling of Combine Generation music, they make apparent its character. International avant-garde styles—as exemplified in America by the works of Cage, Feldman, Carter, and Babbitt, in Germany by Stockhausen and Kagel, in France by Boulez, in Italy by Nono, and in Sweden by Welin—although hardly part of the whistling repertoire of the music devotee, are regarded as "history" by the New Bohemia composer.

In his book *Postface,* Dick Higgins gives an interesting insight into the attitude of the young New Bohemia composer. He says, in effect, that the International Style is all one style: no matter how the style is arrived at and no matter how it is notated, it all comes out sounding the same. He sees the jostling for position between International Style composers as resembling the competition between beer companies. A good summation of the New Bohemia composer's general attitude is Higgins' remark: ". . . musical activity takes place in time, and it seems to me that anything that just breaks up time by happening in it, absorbing it, is musical."

"anything that just breaks up time by happening in it is musical"

The musical activities of the New Bohemia have fastened onto the peripheries of traditional music as we know it. The physical action leading up to the actual playing of a piece, which was traditionally got through as inconspicuously as possible, now may of itself constitute a complete musical composition. Traditional instruments are, more often than not, looked upon as self-sufficient objects, as "characters," or as sound-making entities on a par with a washtub.

The musical action is usually performed in the impromptu style so dear to the hearts of the seekers-of-truth-through-unpredictability. It would seem, in fact, that the more amateur the performance, the more genuine the message—or non-message—behind it. The spectacle of well-trained musicians operating within concepts that force them to be amateur is, to say the least, distressing. The sad truth of the matter is that not only have very few of them that something called stage presence, so essential to the performer, but they are also strikingly lacking in intuition when it comes to conceiving and staging this "music of the environment." With very few exceptions they offer the listener a mélange of pretentiously unpretentious tedium. Of course, there is no question but that the performers are having themselves a ball.

a mélange of pretentiously unpretentious tedium

Again, there is no need to rake up old Dada justifications, since New Bohemia music, literary to the point of no return, is already smothered in verbiage. The movement has a literature that indicates its intent to be historical, not to say significant. And, oddly enough, most of these publications show a concern with professionalism, sophistication of taste, and sleekness of design that might be put to more cogent use in staged productions.

For example, the books of artist Diter Rot, published in Iceland and Germany, function as stunning exercises in both the visual and the literary. (Rot will soon be joining the faculty of Yale University.) New York's Something Else Press, conceived and owned by Dick Higgins, publishes works by New Bohemia composers, writers, and artists: notable recent examples are Al Hansen's *A Primer of Happenings and Time/Space Art,* and artist Ray Johnson's *The Paper Snake.* In matters of typography, photography, and layout, Wolf Vostell's German periodical *Décollage,* devoted to in-depth analysis and celebration of under-

137

ground events, is the last word in the genre. Yoko Ono's *Grapefruit,* published by Wunternaum Press in Bellport, Long Island, has a quaint, Oriental wood-block look, much in keeping with Miss Ono's own word-of-mouth compositions.

These brilliantly executed publications make clear the Combine Generation's passion for the literary and the visual. Another phenomenon makes itself felt, however, after a careful perusal of their contents. The words "purposeless" and "meaningless" appear often and in various guises, seeming to offer an important key to the attitude of New Bohemia composers and artists vis-à-vis their work. In the book *An Anthology,* edited by La Monte Young, designed by George Maciunas (who later began *Fluxus*), and published by Young and Jackson Mac Low in May, 1963, appears an essay by the sculptor Walter de Maria entitled "Meaningless Work." It reads, in part:

"Meaningless work is obviously the most important and significant art form today" Meaningless work is obviously the most important and significant art form today. The aesthetic feeling given by meaningless work can not be described exactly because it varies with each individual doing the work. Meaningless work is honest. Meaningless work will be enjoyed and hated by intellectuals - though they should understand it. Meaningless work can not be sold in art galleries or win prizes in museums. . . . Like ordinary work, meaningless work can make you sweat if you do it long enough. By meaningless work I simply mean work which does not make you money or accomplish a conventional purpose. For instance, putting wooden blocks from one box to another, then putting the blocks back to the original box, back and forth, back and forth etc., is a fine example of meaningless work. . . . Caution should be taken that the work chosen should not be too pleasureable, lest pleasure becomes the purpose of the work.

. . . Try some meaningless work in the privacy of your own room. In fact, to be fully understood, meaningless work should be done alone or else it becomes entertainment for others and the reaction or lack of reaction of the art lover to the meaningless work can not honestly be felt.

Dick Higgins, in his book *Postface,* says:

The nature of purposelessness interests me very much. It is a great source of mental refreshment to do something for no particular reason, especially when it is not interesting or re-freshing. One simply becomes very conscious of nothing in particular. That phenomenon is implicit in a lot of my work.

Behind this striving for purposelessness, meaningless-ness, and indeterminacy is the desire to keep the work—and the mind as well—open, flexible, and free of the pre-conceived. In this way the composer hopes to avoid rigidity of thought, action, or meaning, and presumably to be put into contact with elements that will heighten and deepen his and the audience's responses.

To put it more simply, the New Bohemia composer depends on and makes room for the element of surprise within his compositions—for the performers, for the audi-ence, and for himself. The character of his work usually manifests his wish to make a virtue of the fact that no two performances of *anything* are ever the same. This is in total contrast to electronic music, which relieves us of per-formers as well as of chance.

no two performances of anything are ever the same

Concerts of New Bohemia music occur quite regularly in the East Village. In many instances they are held in lofts; Yoko Ono's loft concerts are frequently mentioned in the literature. Some works were first heard at Miss Ono's Pitt Street loft on the Lower East Side. And the Bridge Theater and Film-Makers' Cinematheque are still the scenes of many such concerts.

This music, more often than not, is far more interesting on the page than in performance. Of the shortcomings of the New Bohemia composer, perhaps the greatest is his intoxication with duration. Another is his sadistic explora-tion of the pain-threshold, via volume and/or agonizing sounds, in order to put the audience through *something*. These experiments are usually gimmicky and uninterest-ing, resembling a calculated inducement of anxiety for its own sake.

These noises, these interminable, yawn-provoking self-indulgences are, at times, alleviated by works of genuine quality. For example, the compositions of George Brecht,

Nam June Paik, and, occasionally, Dick Higgins are frequently exhilarating. When the various components of one of their performances fall into place, the audience can get caught up in an experience that is immediate and arresting.

When all the elements do work, New Bohemia music points, in a curious way, to strong cinematic involvement, although these composers do not generally use film as part of their environmental compositions. But such an orientation becomes evident when we see the relationship between the character of their works and that of the newsreel, with its quick-cutting and splicing of *non sequitur* activities, the unselfconscious, non-acting engrossment of people in these activities, the "nature" sounds that serve as background, and the elements of the unforeseen inherent in all reportage of "life"—that unpredictable, all-inclusive Happening. Within this context, then, the possibilities of cinema still remain a most vital springboard for finding and realizing open-end art forms.

CHAPTER IX

Pushing the Anxiety Button

Omix, presented by Gerd Stern's USCO at the Film-Makers' Cinematheque; the production involved live performers, film, sound tapes, oscillators, and lights

*C*reative New Bohemia's *idée fixe* is group activity. Without it, new theater, new cinema, new music, and new dance could not exist. With the merging of all art forms and the cross-usage of their premises has come a return to the workshop idea, where events are staged to see what will happen "this time." In a sense, offstage has become onstage. Artists of the Combine Generation are also enamored of the notion that excitement and suspense reside in productions that are continually on the brink of not coming off; the element of risk is catnip to them. And the audience, gathered to witness or take part in whatever event, joins with the performers in a mutual "I double dare you."

In addition, a feeling of improvisational games runs rampant in these productions. It is as if these new filmmakers, composers, etc., were trying to make things happen that will recreate and play upon the primacy of a child's total involvement and lay bare the spirit of a child's untrammeled inventiveness. It is not, however, uninhibited artistic play leading to an exuberant end product that engages this Bohemia. What enthralls is the frame and process of continuity in which one "newness" can lead fluidly to another.

Concurrent with the environmental preoccupations of new cinema and new music is the happening. What is a happening? A happening, as the world by now surely knows, is anything that happens, but usually it consists of an environment, created or selected by an artist, in, on, and around which certain skeletally planned events are made to take place. This environment may range from the indoors or outdoors of the city in which the participants live, to the beach, the woods, a highway, or a mountain of discarded rubber tires. The audience becomes the cast. Here, at long last, is the answer for the stagestruck—or, to put it another way, the end of the star system.

Here is a typical happening by Allan Kaprow, the artist credited with having invented the genre:

Here, at long last, is the answer for the stagestruck

MIRRORS—A Happening

Maze of wall size mirrors (as at old-time carneys). Rows of blinking yellow blue and white lights. Quiet neons. Everybody wanders aimlessly. Rubbish on floors in passageways. Five janitors come in with vacuum-sweepers sucking up debris. Crackling sounds. Janitors leave. From above, whistling of some sad pop-tune like "Don't play it no More." More debris is dropped into passageways. Crackling sounds again. Janitors rush around handing out brooms and everybody sweeps. Lots of dust, coughs. Wheelbarrows and shovels rolled in. Frenzied loading of trash, much noise. Brooms are grabbed from people, are held up close to mirrors and examined. Fellow comes in with wide brush and pail of soapy water and wipes over reflections. Janitors sweep and shout at each other from different passageways. *But all their words are backwards.* They yell louder and faster. Then work and noise wears out and finally stops, dust settles, cans of beer are brought in for everybody. Workmen take a swig, burp and pour beer on floor. They go. Dead Silence——. Three pneumatic triphammers are dragged in. Compressors start. Floor is drilled into, noise is deafening, mirrors shatter.

What may be surmised from this and other happenings is that Kaprow has his finger on the anxiety button, and he seldom lets go. Instead of merging the arts, he merges everyday actions and objects chosen for their ordinariness and anxiety potential. He has been creating happenings since 1958, many on a much more epic scale than *Mirrors*.

Kaprow has his finger on the anxiety button, and he seldom lets go

Among other artists who have created happenings are Claes Oldenburg, Robert Whitman, Jim Dine, Red Grooms, and Al Hansen. The works of each of them bear distinct trademarks.

Oldenburg's by now famed "store," on East Second Street in the East Village, was the scene of numerous happenings, not the least of which was the store itself, a rented premises where he sold "food." The food, of course, was made out of plaster, constructed and painted to resemble the real thing. Although most of it was sold quite cheaply over the counter by Oldenburg himself, enacting the storekeeper, some of the pie and cake slices, ice-cream sundaes, hamburgers, hams, etc., may be seen today in elegant

Al Hansen (in mask) appearing in his happening, *Red Dog*, at his Third Rail Gallery

cases at art museums and private collections throughout the country.

The happenings that took place in Oldenburg's store in the late fifties were exercises in enigmatic behavior on the part of "casts" assigned to roles that invariably suggested obsessive, anxiety-ridden states. Members of the audience, who stood around the performance area, were caught up in these happenings like witnesses to irrationally disquieting events.

Nor has the genre changed a great deal. As recently as December, 1965, the Film-Makers' Cinematheque offered an evening of happenings by Oldenburg, Whitman, and Robert Rauschenberg. On this particular evening, seven years after Kaprow had produced the first happening, the basic amalgamation of everyday things, actions, and anxieties was still eminently present.

Oldenburg, ever mindful of the *real* environment, called his jokey happening *Moviehouse*. The audience that had come to see it was asked to stand in the aisles during its performance, while Santa Claus (!), Pat Oldenburg (the artist's wife), and four other people became the audience at a movie theater. This, in effect, constituted the subject matter of the happening. The theater was dark and the projector beamed a rectangle of light onto the red curtain of the stage. The "performers" were fully dressed for winter and laden with afternoon-moviegoing paraphernalia: a surfeit of shopping bags, packages, newspapers, and so forth. They straggled into various rows, compulsively selecting their seats. Once seated, the search for comfort began, as they unburdened themselves of their miscellanies. The action continued with the constant bundling up and transporting of everything to different seats. Two "ushers" enacted a flashlight ritual in perennial search of lost objects in each of the rows. And so it went— the molester, the screaming woman, the coughing, the smoking, the doctor in the house, all to the tune of an inane child's melody played over and over on a piano.

Santa Claus, Pat Oldenburg, and four other people became the audience

147

During Rauschenberg's happening, the *real* audience was finally allowed to be seated. Here was a far more complex event entailing the shifting of word cards to form diverse sentences; an idiotic travelogue film projected on placards worn by the audience; the slow and turgid progress of people, encircled by rubber tires, across the stage and over a bedspring wired for sound, which, under the weight of these paraplegic walkers, made noises like the infernal clanging together of garbage cans; and Rauschenberg himself performing an on-again, off-again, neon-light experiment of great inventiveness. This strange, thoroughly hypnotic happening successfully transformed the banal into the magical, not to say the ominous.

Robert Whitman's part of the program—perhaps more akin to new cinema than to happening—consisted of a wide-screen color film celebrating prestidigitation as implied in the world of fashion. Those who have followed Whitman's career as creator of happenings must have been conscious of the leap from the rags that characterized his earliest efforts to the projected riches of his "magic lantern." This ingenious new work had three chicly slender girls, dressed in white, standing just in front of the movie screen, nearly invisible within the flow of images. Soon, however, the girls themselves became living screens, as the shape and color of their dresses were miraculously changed by the movie images projected onto them.

the happening has become the leitmotif of almost all its creative activities

For the Combine Generation, the happening has become the leitmotif of almost all its creative activities. New theater, new cinema, new music, and new dance all show this. The happening's influence on the new dance may be equated with its effect on the new music. Not only are the creative approaches of one art applied to another, but the artists themselves also exchange roles. It is no longer news that artist Robert Rauschenberg may be seen dancing in recitals given by the Merce Cunningham group. Nor is there news in the fact that Rauschenberg has himself choreographed whole dances, as well as designing sets and

Deborah Hay in Robert Rauschenberg's happening, *Map Room II;* the birdcage contains live pigeons

costumes for them. This is by no means a bid for a new stardom, but simply a natural extension of Rauschenberg's concern with motion, so continually apparent in his work.

In a recent dance recital at the Bridge Theater in the East Village, Trisha Brown came on stage carrying a can of red paint and a brush; she proceeded to employ them, as would a painter, on the backdrop. On the same program was a work entitled *Poem for the Theater #6*. The credits alone give an indication of the combine syndrome at work: Danced by Beverly Schmidt, Conceived by Stephen Tropp (the poet), Filmed by Mario Jorrin, and Directed by Roberts Blossom. Blossom, it should be noted, has been known first as an actor of extraordinary talent, more recently as a director of plays, and presently as the creator of productions based on the integration of art forms.

Poem for the Theater #6, set to music by Villa-Lobos, is an example of what the Combine Generation can accomplish for the dance. Miss Schmidt, garbed in a long red damask dress, danced in front of a wide screen upon which was projected a black-and-white film showing a landscape beyond a stone balustrade. As the film's pace increased—that is, as the image of the now open landscape began to travel by more rapidly—the illusion of a spinning environment was created, and the live dancer seemed to float within it. Throughout, her movements were lyrical, but restrained. Miss Schmidt neither accelerated nor diminished her own movements, but continued to follow the serene dictates of the Villa-Lobos music. As sequence followed sequence, the filmed image went from positive to negative, so that the dancer now seemed to be hovering in a dream landscape. Soon the movements of the camera, which had, up to this moment, been horizontal, became vertical and diagonal, creating an entirely different illusion, one of soaring flight. This counterpoint of motion between dancer and camera created a breathtaking evocation of dreams of flight, with their ambiguous feeling of suspended motion.

a breathtaking evocation of dreams of flight

150

Jill Johnston, long affiliated with avant-garde dance movements and a leading spokesman for the new dance, has written extensively on the subject. In her article "Freedom for Action," published in *The Village Voice,* she makes clear the context out of which the new dance has arisen. The rigors and athleticism of ballet and the modern dance, she claims, have alienated dancers from the possibilities found in natural, everyday movements. The maintenance of academically super-functional bodies has kept them from realizing the body's natural and individual potentialities. Miss Johnston writes:

The idea is not to teach anything, since there is no longer anything to teach, but to encourage the dancers to do whatever they want to do. If they feel like dancing, they'll dance and if they feel like standing on their heads and spitting out nickels, they'll do that, too. Methods of teaching are revealing. Methods are not guide-lines to correct performance. Methods are like road signs at an intersection indicating the possibility of many directions.

"if they feel like standing on their heads and spitting out nickels, they'll do that, too"

The "methods" Miss Johnston speaks of refer to the open-ended teachings of Robert Dunn. The courses in dance composition that he held in New York in 1961 defined new dance and developed into the highly avant-garde Judson Dance Theater.

The Judson Dance Theater originated and continues to function at the Judson Memorial Church on Washington Square, although contingents frequently perform at the Bridge Theater in the East Village. It is that most radical of phenomena, a dance company that has not required the proverbial years of discipline to give it realization. It represents, in fact, a movement in which the word "dance" is usually thought of within invisible quotation marks. Dancers may try anything. They may speak, sing, whistle, grunt, or scream. They may perform actions so far removed from normal expectations as to resemble a kind of calculated stream-of-consciousness assemblage of movements. In effect, new dance is anti-dance (which does not necessarily imply anti-creative or anti-aesthetic dance).

151

The idea of improvisational play in public, a common denominator in most New Bohemia creative activities, is manifested in perhaps its purest form in the new dance. Once again, the unforeseen development is made room for, and the aim is to realize spontaneous creativity and share the pleasure to be found in it.

New dance choreography is used to stimulate the ingenuity of the individual dancer or group of dancers. The dancer is not employed as an automaton executing someone else's ideas, but is expected to "play" freely on the skeletal indications given him by the choreographer. In short, the relationship between dancer and choreographer is invariably one of equality in creative play.

The Judson group has produced a number of startling works, among them Yvonne Rainer's *Terrain* and *Room Service,* Carolee Schneemann's *Noise Bodies,* Viola Farber's *Seconds,* Steve Paxton's *Deposit,* Judith Dunn's *Acapulco,* Alex Hay's *Colorado Plateau,* Lucinda Child's *Geranium,* and Robert Rauschenberg's *Pelican.* Each of these dances is characterized by references to everyday game activities, both juvenile and adult. They may incorporate blown-up sports photographs, dime-store rubber balls, roller skates, etc., and may be performed to taped sounds ranging from traffic noises to football games to poetry readings to radio commercials to the music of Rimsky-Korsakov.

The hazards of failure, even the risks of disaster, are taken for granted by dancer and choreographer, as well as by audience. The attitude is that of children towards their own games; they are aware that in improvised play there is no one "right" way, but rather *many* ways of sustaining pleasure.

This overall sense of freedom does, of course, have its pitfalls. In deliberately forgoing carefully planned productions—which, in the minds of new dancers and choreographers, are synonymous with "commercial" productions—the new dance often falls prey to the same sort of

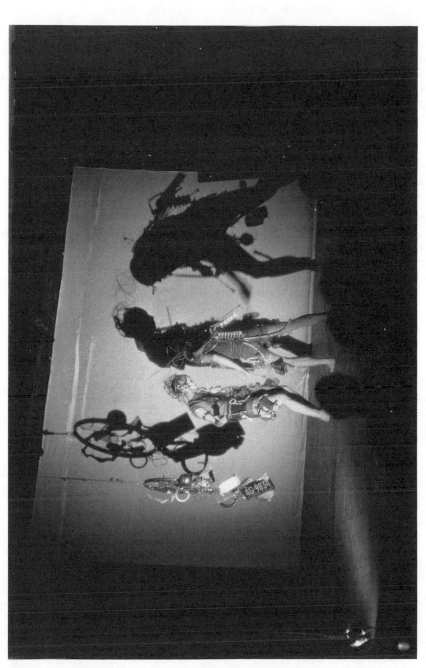

Carolee Schneemann and James Tenney in Miss Schneemann's *Noise Bodies* at the Bridge Theater

redundancy and length that make so much of the new music and the new cinema a study in tedium.

What is more, the new dance can give rise to the most obsessively attenuated indulgences, the kind that border on a fanatic, not to say frantic, concern with the ritual of chance. A dazzling case in point is the form of the new dance invented by Jackson Mac Low, which he calls *dance-instruction-poems*. Based on a chance-composed and chance-selected set of phrases typed on vocabulary cards and describing actions, Mac Low's system is of a complexity that would give Fortuna herself *delirium tremens*. Here is a chance dance-poem from his book entitled *The Pronouns —A Collection of 40 Dances—For the Dancers—6 February– 22 March 1964*:

28TH DANCE—MAPPING—22 March 1964

No-one makes the stomach let itself down,
& no-one is a band or acts like a bee,
& no-one lets an impulse do something through him.

No-one's mapping,
& no-one's paining by going or having waves.

No-one is walking,
& finally, no-one is testing different things.

And here, for those whose obsession threshold is high, are excerpts from Mac Low's "Some Remarks to the Dancers (How the Dances Are to Be Performed & How They Were Made)":

. . . The dances require various numbers of performers. Some are obviously solos or duets, & some will be found to require a group of a definite number that will probably be the same in any realization, but the sizes of the groups required in many of them are somewhat indefinite & are to be decided for each realization by the dancers themselves by careful interpretation of the given text.

In realizing any particular dance, the individual dancer or group of dancers has a very large degree of freedom of interpretation. However, although they are to interpret the successive lines of each of these poems-which-are-also-dance-instructions as they see fit, dancers are required to find *some definite interpretation* of the *meaning* of *every* line of the dance-poems

154

they choose to realize. Above all, no line or series of lines may be left uninterpreted & unrealized simply because it seems too complicated or obscure to realize as movement (&/or sound or speech).

In addition to finding concrete meanings as actions for every line of each dance-poem realized, the dancers must carefully work out the time-relations between the various actions, as indicated by their positions in the poems & by the particular conjunctions & adverbs used to connect them together within the sentence-length strophes, & to connect those strophes together. For example, if a poem indicates that someone "has the chest between thick things *while* he says things about making gardens" a dancer may realize each of these actions as he sees fit, but they must take place simultaneously, *not* one after the other. . . .

Now, as to HOW THEY WERE MADE: The actions of the 40 dances comprised in THE PRONOUNS were drawn by a systematic "chance" method (outlined below) from a "pack" of 56 filing cards, on each of which are typed one to five actions, denoted by gerunds or gerundial phrases, e.g., "jumping," "having a letter over one eye," & "giving the neck a knifing or coming to give a parallel meal, beautiful & shocking." 170 different actions are each named once in this pack of cards, & three more, "jumping," "mapping," & "questioning," are each named twice. (That is, in the 56 sets of one to five actions, there are, in all 176 "places" filled by 173 *different* actions, three of which actions in two of the sets, the rest each only in one.)

" 'coming to give a parallel meal, beautiful & shocking' "

This pack of actions was composed in May 1961. At that time, these 56 sets of one to five actions were typed on another set of filing cards, on each of which one to ten single words were also typed. Both these single words & all the definite lexical words among the words & phrases denoting actions were drawn, with the help of the RAND table of a million random digits, from the 850-word Basic-English Word List. In the action-naming phrases, each Basic-English word was used in any desired form (i.e., as verb, adverb, adjective, or noun, in the singular or the plural, &c.). For example, if I drew the word "beautiful" from the list, I might use it as "beauty," "beautify," "beautiful," "beautifully," "beauties," "beauty's," "beautifying," "beautified," &c. Structure words (conjunctions, prepositions, pronouns, indefinite nouns, &c.) were freely used in connecting these Basic-English "nuclei" into phrases. However, the number & order of succession of the Basic-English "nuclei" in each action-phrase were determined by systematic "chance" although their grammatical form & connections were freely chosen by the author.

155

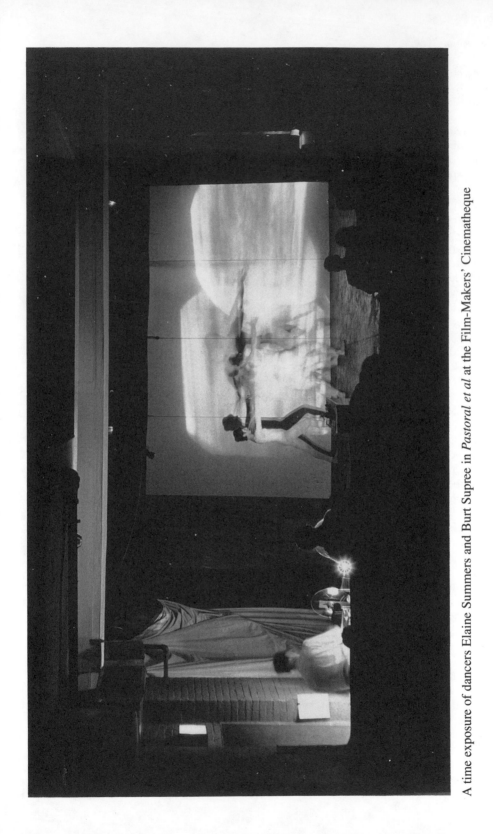

A time exposure of dancers Elaine Summers and Burt Supree in *Pastoral et al* at the Film-Makers' Cinematheque

Mac Low's "Remarks to the Dancers" continue for several paragraphs more, each adding to a verbal quagmire of compulsive proportions. Compared to this incredibly convoluted rationale, the dance-poems themselves are studies in lucidity.

But whether lucid or obscure, the new dance *has* taken its vocabulary from the "Basic-English" of everyday actions. Like its sister arts in the New Bohemia, it wants to demolish the wicked witch of tradition with a "Rubbish, my dear, you have no power here!"

Recitals of the new dance occur with greater and greater frequency and its message is being disseminated more rapidly than one would think. Unlike the heroic dance forms promulgated by such dancer-choreographer-divas as Martha Graham, Doris Humphreys, and Agnes de Mille, the new dance insists on a return to those body actions which are as natural and non-arty as, for example, opening a can of beans or walking a dog. The melodramatic earnestness so prevalent in "modern" dance is shunned like the plague. The new dance wishes to celebrate LIFE in its natural state, unhampered by aesthetic harnesses and unimpeded by mystiques of noble content.

157

CHAPTER X

The New "Professionals": The Celebration of the Unethical Combine

Charlotte Moorman and Nam June Paik in Paik's *Variations on a Theme by Saint-Saens*

*T*he happening boys will latch onto such real-life events as an automobile collision to corroborate their own insistence on unpredictability. It is no mere coincidence that the publication *Décollage* has on the cover of its fourth issue, devoted to happenings, a photograph showing just such an accident. It is described in the inner flap as follows:

SIX PEOPLE KILLED IN A HIGHWAY CRASH

The twisted and bloody body of one dead man dangles through the doorway of a crumpled car and the corpse of his fellow passenger sprawls in the dirt at the rear of the car after an accident on a highway near Pittsburgh, Pa. Three cars and a bus collided at high speed and the sound of the crash could be heard for miles. This accident took the lives of six people and wreckage was strewn for 75 yards along the highway. Police and firemen worked for hours to remove some of the bodies from the mangled wreckage.

The accompanying photograph, so cruelly graphic that only a tabloid would cash in on it, appears with studied casualness on the cover of this organ of the avant-garde. *The real horrors of life are no longer to be ignored in the arts* The real horrors of life are no longer to be ignored in the arts, as is so often demonstrated in happenings that evoke or play on feelings from which we would instinctively turn away. We note how violently the separation between art and life is now attacked, although it was heretofore considered unethical to merge the two without a highly conscious, "artistic" process of transmutation.

In the new cinema, the unethical is represented most obviously by the notion that sex in public is as valid as sex in private. Unabashed sexual exhibitionism via the experimental silver screen is one of this group's favorite ways of flouting traditional ethics. More importantly, however, the new cinema no longer considers the moving screen image as an end product. Its most radical premise is that movement, the most important characteristic of life, can produce a cinematic experience without being confined to film.

The composer of new music thinks nothing either of omitting sound from his compositions altogether, or, conversely, of using sound, pitch, and volume sadistically. Music as the eternal beguiler of the senses, as the sweet assuager of woe, as the merciful embalmer of all care, is as dead as a doornail. King Saul has snatched the lyre from David's hands and plays madly on.

The new dance, the new theater, and the new literature offer similar excursions into the unethical. And then there are the activities of those people whose workaday lives are based on a redefinition of the ethics syndrome. Rev. Alvin Carmines of the Judson Memorial Church on Washington Square fulfills his clerical duties with appropriate conviction, concurrently composing music for some highly unorthodox plays, most of which are presented at the church itself. The lyrics for Rosalyn Drexler's hilarious *Home Movies,* for example, could not by any stretch of the imagination be called pious. And Mr. Carmines' "sporty, bawdy, gaudy" tunes for them were anything but hymnlike. Judson Memorial, under the enlightened guidance of Rev. Howard Moody, has already become known as one of the most forward-looking and liberal churches in the United States. In effect, Messrs. Moody and Carmines are redefining the role, province, and potential of the church in the community.

a redefinition of the ethics syndrome

The same can be said for the activities of Saint Mark's-in-the-Bouwerie, the three-hundred-year-old church on East Tenth Street and Second Avenue. This exquisitely proportioned house of worship, a focal landmark of the East Village, is the oldest religious site on Manhattan that has been in continuous use. Lying buried within its grounds are Peter Stuyvesant, Daniel Tompkins, and Commodore Perry. In the summer months, far-out jazz combos play over their heads, in a setting that abounds with the sort of wild sculpture that makes passersby do a series of double takes.

Within the walls of the church, "Theater Genesis" holds forth. Here again nothing is sacred as far as language and subject are concerned. As Rev. Thomas Pike, formerly of

163

Saint Mark's-in-the-Bouwerie

Saint Mark's, put it, "The search that an artist experiences in the process of creating something—the human struggle for ultimate understanding—is inherently religious."

Thus, what may seem unethical, let alone shocking, to the average churchgoer, is, in the minds of certain churchmen, a matter of desirability if not paramount importance. While there is no denying the frequent shock elements to be found in the theatrical productions of both the Judson Memorial Church and Saint Mark's—productions, incidentally, which do not ride on the prurient but often wittily satirize it—these are condoned and supported in a spirit of affirmation, almost as if these churches wished to realign themselves creatively with life as it is and move out of their millstone area of negative righteousness.

unethical, let alone shocking

Another example of the unethical combine is provided by the director-critic who reviews his own directorial stint, and the playwright-critic who reviews his own play. Both breaches in "etiquette" were committed by one Michael Smith, an unusually perceptive young drama critic, a talented playwright, and a fledgling director. Smith himself, in his *Village Voice* column, has made a definite point of questioning the moral assumptions of this *modus operandi*. After a lengthy and astute critique of the Albert Marre production of *Man of La Mancha*, presented last season at the ANTA Washington Square Theatre, he launches into a review of *Icarus's Mother*, a play that he himself directed for production at the Caffe Cino. The author of the play is Sam Shepard, one of the bright lights on the Off-Off-Broadway scene. Smith, with the sensibilities of a good critic, reviews the play's content and then candidly proceeds to pan the work of the director. In so doing, he publicly analyzes his own failings, all the while retaining his objective distance.

Smith goes into the matter of ethics in the introduction to his review, and his words are eminently worth quoting:

I have devoted most of my organized energy over the past six weeks to a production at the Cafe Cino of Sam Shepard's

165

one-act play "Icarus's Mother." In recent tradition the critic has become an outsider, a representative of the audience who views the finished product and judges its merit. Such a role is not only uncomfortable but also dull. The critic tends to become an enemy of the theater rather than its ally, and his implicit identification with the generalized audience point of view is depersonalizing and false. . . . I have tried to define a different role for the critic. I write plays as well as reviews, many of my friends are active in the theater (acting, writing, directing, designing lights, etc.), and my reviews are basically addressed to the artist. By discussing the work in terms of its creation, rather than the "objective" terms of the judge, I provide one side of a hopeful dialogue. My side is certainly less important than that being created in action by the theater artists themselves. Theater consists of the playwright writing, the director conducting rehearsals, the designers preparing the physical production, and the actors performing in the presence of an audience. The critic is extraneous and largely useless in all of this and has, in our present pseudo-theater become little more than an unpredictable but necessary publicist.

Apart from the discomfort of this isolation, I have felt often that I simply didn't know what I was talking about, I can discuss playwrighting because I know what it feels like to write a play. But otherwise I have little experience in the theater. . . . I don't really know what it's like to cast a play, rehearse it, and participate in its performance. This lack of knowledge and involvement along with the sheer quantity of theater I see, tends to make me go dead, lose my responsiveness and passion, and thus cease to be effective or happy as a critic.

With all of this in mind, I have directed a play for the Judson Poet's Theater, assisted in lighting several plays and dance concerts, persisted writing plays of my own, appeared on stage at the Cafe Au Go Go, and participated in the experimental activities of the Open Theater. Although I am aware of the dangers—partisanship, a loss of critical distance, prejudice for or against my friends, etc.—I hope to continue in this direction and to review plays as a man of the theater rather than a journalist on the theater beat.

Smith, in reviewing *More! More! I Want More!*, a play done at the Cafe La Mama which he wrote in collaboration with two other authors, was short and to the point: "I thought it was perfect," was the single comment.

A further example of the probing of the outrageous occurred at New York's Bonino Gallery when Nam June Paik offered an exhibition that explored electronics, using everyday television fare as a basis for art. Electronics was given reverential treatment by Paik, who filled the gallery with innumerable TV sets, each of them "prepared" so that the images on the screens assumed new visual significance.

Each TV screen showed splendid distortions of regular programs. Sound was equally distorted. The result was an audacious tampering with the miracle of electronics as a medium of communication. Paik is convinced that the tampered-with television tube will eventually serve artists as has the canvas.

But, not satisfied with the mere obliteration of an invention that has taken scientists years to bring into dubious focus, the Korean artist also elected to create a super-robot. There is, of course, nothing new in this, except that robot-making has usually been the province of scientists. Where Paik and the scientists differ is in the matter of electronic scrambling. Paik's six-foot robot, seen walking and talking at the Bonino Gallery, was controlled by a twenty-channel radio transmitter, a ten-channel data recorder, a video tape recorder, three television cameras, and twenty-three cathode-ray screens. All of the circuits had been revised or invented by the artist.

Actually, Paik's electronic fiddle-faddling is not half so interesting as are his live performances. In a composition seen at the Film-Makers' Cinematheque, for example, a simultaneous combination of film, live music, and strip-tease was given an imaginatively conceived and carefully integrated once-over. The star of the piece was cellist Charlotte Moorman, who served as both cello soloist and stripper. In effect, the audience saw short segments of a film by Robert Breer, alternating with a view of Miss Moorman, live, silhouetted by backlighting behind the projection screen, playing short phrases of a Bach cello sonata. Each time a phrase was completed, Miss Moorman removed a piece of clothing. Once the piece of clothing was dropped, the lights behind the screen were turned off

Charlotte Moorman served as both cello soloist and stripper

167

and the Breer film immediately flashed on again. This procedure continued until Miss Moorman had dropped her last garment and the performance concluded with a silhouetted view of her lying flat on the floor, amorously playing her cello, which was now on top of her.

This combine performance dreamed up by Nam June Paik ingeniously illustrates how the juxtaposition of live and filmed images, of front and rear projection of light, could make for avant-garde entertainment of the first order.

Among the large cast of characters of the New Bohemia, the charming Miss Moorman has proven to be an entrepreneuse of quite dizzying proportions. Like pianist David Tudor before her, Miss Moorman can perform music of the most savage complexity, or employ her cello in a manner that would give Stradivarius acute apoplexy. What is more, she is an undaunted publicist and protagonist of the new music. Her activities of a single day might include delivering publicity material to the major New York newspapers, organizing festivals of avant-garde music, arranging for the transportation of sundry equipment needed for concerts of new music, handling a barrage of correspondence to and from the various continents where new music is performed, studying and selecting manuscripts to be added to her repertoire, and preparing to perform the same evening. How does Charlotte Moorman earn a living? Sandwiched in between her avant-garde activities, she plays with Leopold Stokowski's American Symphony Orchestra.

Called the "Jeanne d'Arc of New Music" by one of the pioneers of avant-garde music, the late Edgard Varèse, Miss Moorman hails from Little Rock, Arkansas. Like many of her Combine Generation contemporaries, she is thoroughly educated in her field: a student of Leonard Rose at the Juilliard School, she holds bachelor's and master's degrees in music. She has traveled extensively in Europe, winning critical acclaim for her premieres of works by John Cage, Earle Brown, and Karlheinz Stockhausen among many others. "I would give anything to have been the first to perform Brahms's *Double Concerto*," says the cellist. "Since I couldn't do that, I am satisfied and thrilled to play the newest and most exciting music of our time. In fact, it's what I live for."

Miss Moorman's performance in a recent concert at Judson Hall, witnessed by many an astonished eye, required her to swathe her naked self in Saran Wrap and jump into a tub of water, part of Nam June Paik's musical composition, *Variations on a Theme by Saint-Saëns*. Taking off one's clothes before the public as part of a serious musical composition is not exactly accepted concert-hall deportment—not yet, anyway. But Miss Moorman and Paik are paving the way with considerable eloquence.

Another of the New Bohemia's high priestesses was the late Countess Ruth Landshoff von Yorck, or, as she preferred to be called, Ruth Yorck. "I am rediscovered every year," she used to say in a soft German accent, "but, like Persephone, I always return underground."

Yet Ruth Yorck, keenly intelligent and ever responsive, did venture aboveground in many avatars. If she was not as well known as she surely deserved to be, it is because she refused to concentrate on one existence. Disdaining the role of either celebrity or queen bee of the arts, she had, nonetheless, been both at different times in her life. A veteran of various Bohemias, she found her natural ambience among the young playwrights, artists, filmmakers, and poets of the Village, East and West. Her alliance with the Combine Generation was manifested in her plays, which were frequently performed at the Cafe La Mama and the Caffe Cino; in her poetry; which appeared in several underground publications; and in her general moral support of all things experimental.

A veteran of various Bohemias

German by birth, Ruth Yorck passed her childhood among celebrities. On the croquet lawn of her family home, she was surrounded by the likes of Thomas Mann, Gerhart Hauptmann, and Hugo von Hofmannsthal. As a

169

Ruth Yorck died on January 19, 1966, the day after she sat for this portrait

young woman, she was a frequent guest in the homes of Marlene Dietrich, Charlie Chaplin, Arturo Toscanini, Oskar Kokoschka, and Jean-Paul Sartre. *Klatsch, Ruhm und kleine Feuer* (Applause, Fame, and a Small Fire), a volume of recollections published in Germany in 1963, includes first-hand impressions of these, as well as of Jean Cocteau, Carson McCullers, Robert Flaherty, André Gide, Yvette Guilbert, John Latouche, F. W. Murnau, the Countess Polignac, Max Reinhardt, Pavel Tchelitchew, Paul Valéry, Thornton Wilder, and Orson Welles.

These encounters, brief or lengthy, chart Miss Yorck's highly personal path through the various worlds in which she took an active part. In 1922, for example, she made her screen debut in Murnau's *Nosferatu*, a German film classic often revived at the Film-Makers' Cinematheque, and she had an important role in Carl Dreyer's *Die Gezeichnete* (The Marked). Miss Yorck jokingly referred to herself as the Baby Jane Holzer of the twenties; she had, indeed, been the beautiful darling of Berlin, the bewitching and stimulating sprite whose presence in a Viennese *Schloss,* a Venetian *palazzo,* or a Parisian *palais* invariably spelled excitement.

While Ruth Yorck led a legendary life, it was hardly a source of intoxication to her. Others, however, have been obsessed with creating their own legends in their own time. Negro writer LeRoi Jones has left the New Bohemia and, reportedly, his white wife and two children, intent on accomplishing this mission. Until recently a resident of the East Village, Jones had been one of the area's best known playwrights and poets. Although he achieved fame and notoriety with his plays, *Dutchman, The Toilet,* and *The Slave,* Jones has removed himself from the New Bohemia for a role on a wider stage as racial activist, apparently believing that only through hatred, bloodshed, and violence can the Negro achieve equality, if not supremacy.

To create a calculated chaos while keeping a cool head has ever been LeRoi Jones's creative aim. His plays bear

To create a calculated chaos while keeping a cool head

171

LeRoi Jones

witness to this. But his toying with madness—playing, in effect, upon the schizophrenia potential of others, as though it were a medium for personal expression—might be looked upon as a grandiose misapplication of the Combine Generation's prevailing objective of destroying barriers in every direction. The basic difference, of course, is that the Combine Generation uses madness to widen the range of sensibilities; Jones is also battling for the destruction of obsolete ideas, but for him, if he is taken literally, killing the idea requires killing the person.

Thus Jones would seem to recognize and support in daily life Artaud's Theater of Cruelty, which, if imagined to its furthest limits, would mean actual bloodshed and death. To Jones, the theater of cruelty is daily life. However harrowing his ideas may seem from other points of view, Jones—within the context of his message and within the context of the unethical combine—sees no boundaries between art and the realities of everyday existence.

CHAPTER XI

The Epidemic Rash of Irrationality

Dick Higgins' happening, *The Tart*, performed in a boxing ring

*T*here is no doubt that, looked at coldly and calmly, the New Bohemia is berserk. The great, unknown, and forbidding territory of insanity is being tapped as a natural resource—not in quest of sickness, but in quest of an expanded idea of sanity.

The Combine Generation, in its life and in its art, questions the confines of so-called sane behavior, as well it might. It has taken a good look around and decided that *that* system hasn't worked. The results have been a frantic reexamination of all areas of experience and the overthrow of preconceived notions of what life and art are all about. The mergers want a new view of the world, if not a new world. They want to explore a non-finite universe.

If their behavior and their art forms often have about them the look of madness, it is because the New Bohemians have unwittingly discovered the intensity that resides in the mad. It is not the madness itself, but this intensity, this perilously heightened catharsis of experience that they wish to use.

Thus the drug syndrome among the non-addicted, the spasmodic violence of their social dancing, and the prevailing unkemptness of their appearance; all, by now, are minor but obvious characteristics of New Bohemia the world over.

What is less obvious, but far more central to creative New Bohemia, is the way this sense of derangement is used. In cinema, music, theater, dance, literature, and happening, it is calculatedly employed to shatter the habitual and the predictable—not, it should quickly be added, in the manner of the Surrealists with their incredibly operatic depiction of the drama of the great unconscious, but simply by combining the disparate elements of the world as it is. The Combine Generation has *had it* with the probing of the unconscious. It has also *had it* with the overtly symbolic. Again, although the Combine Generation

178

may have embraced Dada's sense of fluidity and invention, it has denied Dada's negativism and anti-art premises. Improvisations, ready-mades, junk art, and Schwitters' holy trivia have all served as source material for the current movement and all have been revealed as obvious adjuncts to the creative process. But it is only in combination that they have relevant meaning for the New Bohemia. In themselves they are no longer revolutionary; they are, rather, historical, because they represent static end products.

If the combining of the arts has taken on the lunatic aspects of a juggling act in an occupational-therapy ward, it is because the mergers want the "action" never to stop. They are enamored of the daily magic rituals; they are obsessed by the repetition of these banal rituals and the time it takes to perform them. It is no longer *space* that must be filled with *things;* now *time* must be filled with *movement.* Time and movement have become the magic binding medium that makes it possible to mix the arts.

To sustain movement is to sustain life. As soon as movement, no matter how imperceptible, stops, *rigor mortis* of meaning sets in. And so fluidity, usually regarded as ephemeral, becomes concrete; the traditionally concrete—art as object or artifact, for example—becomes elusive and perishable. The Combine Generation cannot bear the finality and the confines of static end products; but because they exist as part of the environment and because they serve as the stationary components that define the existence of movement in space, they may be incorporated in order to reveal and stress not only their elusiveness but also their passivity and impotence.

The Combine Generation cannot bear the finality and the confines of static end products

Like surf-riding, the Combine Generation's attitude towards the arts has certain built-in hazards. Unless the riders exercise superb judgment, balance, timing, flexibility, and extraordinary acumen, they are unlikely to make it to shore standing up. So, the New Bohemia's creative activities also look mad because, in truth, they are still in a primitive state.

While everything seems to point towards an inevitable combine of the arts, no supremely successful surf-riders have as yet made their appearance. Undoubtedly they will, and then we shall have more beauty, purity, and form to rebel against. *That* rebellion might lead to a "revolutionary" splintering of the arts by which painting, sculpture, literature, music, theater, dance, and cinema will rediscover their individual virtues, and, indeed, rediscover untapped possibilities within the frameworks that are currently being rejected.

In the meantime the Combine Generation, in the East Village and elsewhere, is frantically busy injecting chaos into our so-called order. Having discovered that the rash of irrationality is incurable, they are attempting to treat it as a thing of beauty and a joy forever.

They may be right.

A Map
of The
East Village

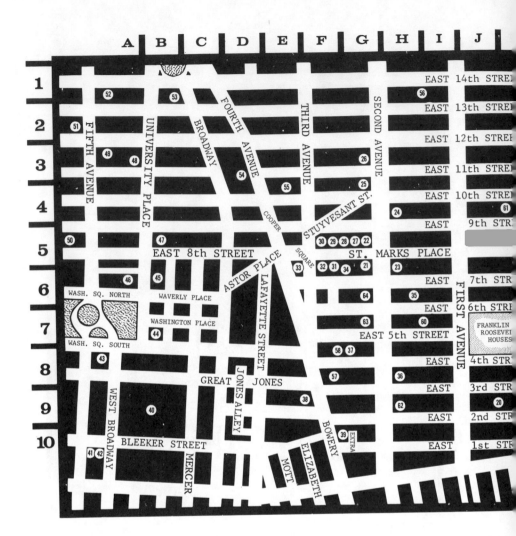

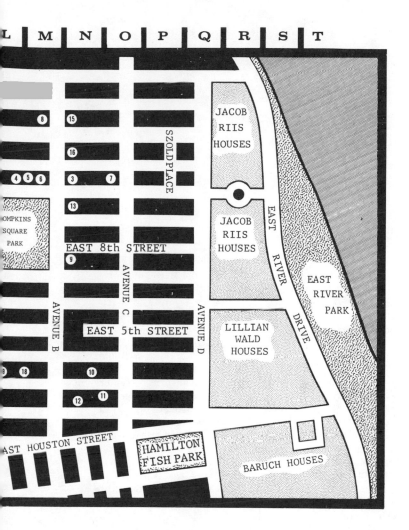

L M N O P Q R S T

SZOLD PLACE

JACOB RIIS HOUSES

EAST RIVER DRIVE

TOMPKINS SQUARE PARK

EAST 8th STREET

JACOB RIIS HOUSES

EAST RIVER PARK

AVENUE C

AVENUE B

EAST 5th STREET

AVENUE D

LILLIAN WALD HOUSES

EAST HOUSTON STREET

HAMILTON FISH PARK

BARUCH HOUSES

Index

184

186

About the Author

John Gruen in the 1960s. Photograph by
Jane Wilson

John Gruen has been writing on art, music, and
dance for over 30 years. In the early 1960s, he
served as a music and art critic for the *New York
Herald Tribune,* a position he held until the paper
folded in 1969. He is the author of *People Who
Dance, The Private World of Leonard Bernstein,
The Party's Over Now,* among others, and the
forthcoming biography, *Keith Haring: Radiant
Child.* He is a Senior Editor of *Dance Magazine,*
and has served as Contributing Editor to *ARTNews
Magazine. The New Bohemia* was his first
published book.

About the Photographer

Fred W. McDarrah in 1964.

Fred W. McDarrah, a native New Yorker, WW II
Paratrooper, NYU Journalism graduate, won a
Guggenheim Fellowship in photography and has
been a photographer and the picture editor of *The
Village Voice* for over three decades. He does
book reviews for *The Picture Professional,* and is
the author of *The Beat Scene, The Artist's World,
Greenwich Village, Museums in New York,
Kerouac & Friends,* and several photography
reference books. McDarrah's photographs have
been exhibited widely.